T0210023

DYNAMIC STUDIES
IN COLOSSIANS AND PHILEMON

BRINGING GOD'S WORD TO LIFE

FRED A. SCHEEREN

WESTBOW
PRESS®
A DIVISION OF THOMAS NELSON
& ZONDERVAN

Scripture quotations marked GNT are taken from the Good News Translation® (Today's English Version, Second Edition). Copyright © 1992 American Bible Society. All rights reserved.

Scripture quotations marked KJV are taken from the King James Version. Public domain.

Scripture quotations marked NIV are taken from The Holy Bible, New International Version®, NIV® Copyright © 1973, 1978, 1984, 2011 by Biblica, Inc.® Used by permission. All rights reserved worldwide.

Scripture quotations marked NKJV are taken from the New King James Version®. Copyright © 1982 by Thomas Nelson. Used by permission. All rights reserved.

Scripture quotations marked NLT are taken from the Holy Bible, New Living Translation, copyright © 1996, 2004, 2015 by Tyndale House Foundation. Used by permission of Tyndale House Publishers, Inc., Carol Stream, Illinois 60188. All rights reserved.

WestBow Press books may be ordered through booksellers or by contacting:

WestBow Press
A Division of Thomas Nelson & Zondervan
1663 Liberty Drive
Bloomington, IN 47403
www.westbowpress.com
1 (866) 928-1240

Because of the dynamic nature of the Internet, any web addresses or links contained in this book may have changed since publication and may no longer be valid. The views expressed in this work are solely those of the author and do not necessarily reflect the views of the publisher, and the publisher hereby disclaims any responsibility for them.

Any people depicted in stock imagery provided by Getty Images are models, and such images are being used for illustrative purposes only.
Certain stock imagery © Getty Images.

ISBN: 978-1-9736-3940-4 (sc)
ISBN: 978-1-9736-3939-8 (e)

Library of Congress Control Number: 2018910902

Print information available on the last page.

WestBow Press rev. date: 10/05/2018

DEDICATION

I DEDICATE THIS book to my lovely wife, Sally, who is a Jewish believer and Ivy League educated attorney. She has stood by me over the years and raised our sons in our God-loving home. The comfort of sharing our friendship and our love for Christ has encouraged me greatly in creating this series of dynamic studies of various books of the Bible. Sally's participation in our small group studies has added a much deeper dimension of richness to the discussions. Thank you for sharing your heritage, training, and knowledge.

CONTENTS

ACKNOWLEDGMENTS

MY FRIEND, BOB Mason, who at the time I began the Dynamic Bible Studies series was in his second career as the pastor of small groups at the Bible Chapel in the South Hills of Pittsburgh, suggested the overall structure of each study. Realizing our group was doing more in-depth work than most, he asked that I include several important segments in each lesson—most specifically, the warm-up and life application phases.

Bob suggested a great resource called the *New Testament Lesson Planner* from InterVarsity Press. I have augmented this with commentaries by Dr. Charles Missler from Koinonia House, the *Wiersbe Bible Commentary*, *The MacArthur Bible Handbook* by Dr. John MacArthur, the *Bible Commentaries* of J. Vernon McGee, and the whole of Scripture itself. To make the utilization of the whole of Scripture more efficient, I have also leaned heavily on the Libronix Digital Library, perhaps the most advanced Bible software available, and other resources to help us understand how the New Testament and the Tanakh (Old Testament) fit together as one cohesive document.

I have also enjoyed the input and encouragement of my friend, Ron Jones, as I have continued to prepare these studies. Ron is a former high school principal and administrator. He is also a committed believer and daily student of God's Word.

His background in education coupled with his love of God and His Word has made him a powerful force for good.

I would also like to express thanks to my good friend, Gordon Haresign, for his continued support and encouragement in my efforts to produce the Dynamic Bible Studies series. Gordon's journey began with his birth in the Belgian Congo. In the following years he was a senior executive with an international accounting firm, served in the military, labored as a Bible college professor, was instrumental in the leadership of a worldwide Bible correspondence school, and currently serves on the board of directors of Scripture Union, an international Bible-based ministry. Gordon's work as a teacher, speaker, and missionary has taken him to over 50 countries on five continents. His two most recent books, *Authentic Christianity* and *Pray for the Fire to Fall* should be required reading for all believers. Speaking of the Dynamic Bible Studies series he has written "These are among the finest, if not the finest, inductive Bible studies available today. I strongly endorse them."

I would also like to express my appreciation to my two proof-readers. This includes:

- Cynthia Nicastro, an intelligent, ardent and devoted student of the Scriptures and a meticulous grammarian.

- My wife Sally, a Jewish believer and Ivy League educated lawyer who was law review in law school, worked for the Superior Court of the State of Pennsylvania, and is now in private practice.

May God bless you, inspire you, teach you, and change your life for the better as you work through these lessons.

PREFACE

Welcome to what I hope you find to be a most enjoyable and enlightening study of two letters written by one of the most intelligent and educated men in history. This man's life was changed from that of a religious zealot to one of the most dedicated followers of the Jewish Messiah. These letters are part of the group of documents that today is known as "The Bible" and are referred to as the Books of Colossians and Philemon.

As we consider how these books of the Bible fits into the whole of the New Testament and the Tanakh (the name used by Jews for the Old Testament, used here to emphasize the Jewishness of the Scriptures), we need to realize a number of things. We should stand in awe of this collection of 66 books, written over thousands of years by at least 40 different authors. Every detail of the text is there by design. It explains history before it happens, and comes to us from outside the dimension of time. It is, in short, the most amazing, most authenticated, and most accurate book available in the world.

If this claim is not strong enough, add to it the indisputable fact that the words contained therein have changed more lives than any others now in existence.

While the Judeo-Christian Scriptures are demonstrably perfect, my prepared studies are not. There is no way I or anyone else could possibly incorporate the depth of the text into individual sessions. I simply desire to provide a vehicle for others to use in their investigation of the Scriptures as they incorporate these timeless truths into their lives.

Speaking of small groups, Dr. Chuck Missler, a former Fortune 500 CEO, said "I experienced more growth in my personal life as a believer by participating in small group Bible studies than anything else." I believe you may find this to be true in your experience and encourage you to be an active participant in such a mutually supportive, biblically-based group.

GROUND RULES

I DESIGNED THE first portion of each study to encourage readers to think about their personal situation. I designed the second portion to help people understand what the text says and how it relates to the whole of Scripture. And finally, each lesson ends with a discussion designed to help people apply that lesson.

You will notice that, in most instances, I have included the citation, but not the actual text of the Scripture we are considering. I did this on purpose. I believe we all learn more effectively if we have to dig out the text itself. As a byproduct of that exercise, we become more familiar with this marvelous book.

Scripture references are preceded or followed by a question or series of questions. Again, this is on purpose. I have also found that people seem to learn most effectively when employing the Socratic Method. That is, instead of telling someone what the text says and how it relates to other texts and life, they will remember it better if they answer questions about it and ferret out the information for themselves.

In a few instances, I have inserted additional commentary or partial answers to some of the questions to help the group get the most out of the study.

It is my intention and suggestion that the various scripture references be read out loud as part of each session. Shorter passages might be read by one participant, while anything over two or three verses might serve everyone better if one member reads one verse and another reads the next until the passage is completed. This keeps everyone involved. After reading these passages, I intend that how they relate to the primary Scripture at hand in Colossians or Philemon be seriously considered. At times, this relationship seems to be available and obvious on the surface. In many other instances, the interconnectedness of the whole of Scripture and its principles are most effectively understood through deeper thought, discussion, and prayer.

In commenting on and discussing the various passages, questions, concepts, and principles in this material, it is not required that any particular person give his or her input. The reader of any passage may, but is not pressured to, give his or her thoughts to the group. This is a group participation exercise for the mutual benefit of all involved and many people in the group giving their insight into a certain verse or question will often enhance the learning experience.

I also have two practical suggestions if you work through this book in a small group setting. Every time you meet, I suggest you review the calendar and agree upon the next scheduled meeting as well as who will bring refreshments. This will help the group to run a lot more smoothly while enhancing everyone's enjoyment and expectations.

INTRODUCTION TO COLOSSIANS

Welcome to a study of the books of Colossians. While this book was written many years ago the issues dealt with are the same ones facing us today. It is as contemporary as if penned last week. This book of the Bible is actually a letter from the Apostle Paul to the believers in the City of Colossae. It was sent to assist them in successfully addressing important questions about faith, life, God and philosophy.

Colossae was one of three cities in the Lycus Valley. It was only 9 miles from Laodicea, the city famous for the letter written to the church there by Jesus Christ himself (see Revelation 3:14-21). This was located in Asia Minor, which is incorporated into present day Turkey. Colossae is thought to have derived its name from The Collosus of Rhodes, one of the seven wonders of the ancient world. This enormous statue was 110 feet high on a 50 foot base and depicted *Helios*, the ancient god of the sun. It was made of the melted and recast enemy weapons left behind when the forces of Ptolemy, one of Alexander the Great's former generals, fought off an invading force led by Demetrius that included 40,000 men and 200 warships. The statue was completed in 280 B.C. and toppled in an earthquake in 224 B.C. The pieces of this great statue lay on the ground for approximately 900 years and were transported to Syria on 900 camels in 656 A.D. when the Arabs conquered the region.

Colossae was essentially situated on a crossroads between the eastern and western worlds. As such, it was known for its fusion of various religious influences including Judaism, Gnosticism, various pagan religions, and even an unusual angel cult. This particular angel cult venerated the archangel Michael who they worshipped and claimed he caused a particular spring with curative powers to gush from the earth. The confluence of these various religious influences was the background, or perhaps the field of weeds into which the Gospel of the Jewish Messiah was introduced.

Paul wrote the letter to the Colossians around 60 A.D. when he was imprisoned in Rome. While it appears that Paul never visited the city itself, he had a deep concern for its people. (See Colossians 1:7, Colossians 2:2, and Colossians 4:12) The group of believers in Colossae was an outgrowth of the time Paul spent in Ephesus. (See Acts 19, 20:17-38) In fact, the witness of the group of believers in Ephesus was so effective that "people throughout the province of Asia—both Jews and Greeks—heard the Lord's message." (Acts 19:10 NLT) Two particular men, Epaphras and Philemon, who were in Ephesus seem to have been primarily responsible for founding the church in Colossae. (See Colossians 1:7)

Philemon actually hosted a group of believers that met in his home (Philemon 1:2). It is felt that Apphia was his wife and Archippus was his son with Archippus serving as the leader of this "church." This particular group of believers seems to have generally been comprised of Gentile converts. (See Colosians 1:25-29 and Colossians 3:5-9) This was a relatively new group and had been in existence for only about 5 years when Paul wrote his letter.

Thus we see the letter of Paul to the believers in Colossae as an effort to help them deal with their confusing environment and the pervasive cultural ideas to which they were continually subjected. He does this in an interesting fashion.

In fact, the method he used is the same as the one used today to assist bank employees in recognizing counterfeit currency. Such employees do not attend classes merely on the production, design and nuances of counterfeit bills so that they can hopefully recognize them when they see them. Instead, they study real money to learn what it looks like, what it feels like, what it smells like, and how it is designed. Having mastered the knowledge of real bills it becomes a much simpler task to recognize a fake when they see it.

Paul was writing to help believers understand the truth of the Scriptures and apply them to their lives. He knew that when they mastered the truth they would be inoculated against heretical or even demonic systems of thought that they might encounter. This problem of discerning truth from lies has been one with which people have had to deal from time immemorial. It even crept into the career of Norman Shelby. Norman Shelby? Who was he and what does this have to do with our discussion you might ask. Norman was a great boxer in the 1800s. However when he found that his name didn't command the respect he sought he changed it to Charles "Kid" McCoy.

Kid McCoy only weighted about 160 pounds, but reportedly packed a tremendous punch. In Fact, when Ring Magazine ranked the 100 greatest punchers of all time in 1957 they included Norman in the group. After "Kid" McCoy began putting together a string of victories in the ring other boxers began to emulate him and even began calling themselves Kid McCoy, just like Norman. In an effort to differentiate himself from these pretenders Norman began to call himself "The Real McCoy." Since then the term "The Real McCoy" has been used to designate things that are genuine or legitimate. This is exactly what Paul was doing in the world of spiritual warfare. He wanted the Colossians to personally know and understand "The Real McCoy," as revealed in Jesus Christ himself and the Judeo Christian Scriptures which we call The Bible.

In our study of Colossians we will attempt to imitate Paul and understand the real thing, the Real McCoy, if you will. To make things a bit easier I have included information on the various pagan and heretical influences with which Paul and the Colossians had to deal. However, our focus, like Paul's, will be upon the truth. Following this you will find a brief summary of a few of the problematic heresies and pagan influences against which Paul, the early believers, and we today have needed to guard.

Gnosticism

The roots of Gnosticism were already apparent in the teachings of some people at the time of the writing of this letter, although it was not more fully developed and recognized until the next century. These people felt that they were the "spiritual aristocracy" and possessed special knowledge. They were arrogant in their unsubstantiated and unprovable heretical theological positions which were quite similar to those embedded in the New Age movement today. They:

- Were attracted to Old Testament dietary laws and ceremonies as a means to attain perfection.

- Adhered to the worship of angels as mediators between human beings and God.

- Claimed that while Jesus was important He was just a man.

- Taught that matter was evil.

- Adhered to a strange form of astrology.

- Felt that good and evil were derived from rules and regulations.

Asceticism

This religious philosophy has many similarities to the "eastern" religions and is almost somewhat ethereal in nature. Those adhering to Asceticism taught that:

- Matter is not evil.

- The human body is not evil.

- Human nature wishes to use the body for evil but since Jesus came as a man the body itself cannot be evil.

- Diets and spiritual discipline are good for a person but cannot develop the "true spirituality" that they sought.

- This somewhat nebulous "true spirituality" is the state to which a "spiritual person" should strive.

Syncretism

This philosophy is pre-eminent in the culture today. It shares many characteristics with secular humanism and is easily recognized in the COEXIST movement. In the end it holds that:

- Everyone's truth is equally valid.

- All peoples of different ideologies ought to get along and accept the validity of everyone else's position on all spiritual matters.

- Everything is acceptable.

- There is therefore no discernable objective truth.

Religious Syncretism is a favorite position of people who like to study "religion," with this "religion" having no real impact upon their lives. Adherents strangely enough may include collegiate religion departments, professors and people who want to feel good because they are "spiritual." They often dabble in or support Buddhism, Hinduism, Islam and other "isms" with no real understanding of what they are doing. Interestingly, they become their own arrogant "gods" in that they are on an individual basis the supreme arbiters of what they consider to be real, right, wrong, true or false.

While the other extra-biblical heresies and modes of thought one encounters in a search for truth are simply misleading, Syncretism is the most outlandishly ridiculous. Adherents to this form of thought claim to be the most open minded of all people but in fact end up as the most closed minded since they feel that everyone who does not agree with them is not only wrong, but that intellectual conversation about "truth" is impossible since it really does not exist.

As mentioned earlier, there is really only one objective answer to the heresies that have misled people. That answer is Jesus Christ as revealed in the historically reliable and demonstrably inerrant and infallible Scriptures of the New and Old Testaments. He alone has provided a way for every person to experience eternal life as well as a worthwhile life now by enabling those who have transgressed against God's moral law (this would be every living person) to be reconciled to God. And, His sacrifice alone, when fully understood, enables one to live a full life now through the power of the Holy Spirit.

Larry Norman has been called the Father of Christian Rock and Roll. When touring in Australia in the 1970's he was asked how he became a religious person. He said "I'm not a religious boy." The interviewer was somewhat surprised and obviously quite skeptical. He said: "You're not?" Larry replied: "No, I have a relationship with Jesus. This is all about a relationship with Jesus Christ as revealed in the Bible and having him as Lord of my life."

Larry's simple statement sums it up well. It is all about a relationship with Jesus Christ, Yeshua Ha-Maschiach, the Jewish Messiah. This privilege can be ours too.

As it says in Colossians 2:3, "In him lie hidden all the treasures of wisdom and knowledge." NLT

WEEK 1

A REMARKABLE LETTER FROM PRISON
COLOSSIANS 1:1-14

Open in Prayer

Group Warm-Up Questions

When was the last time you received a letter from a stranger?

When was the last time you received a letter that really cheered you up? Please explain.

Read: Colossians 1:1-14

What does Paul tell his readers about his current imprisonment in the opening to his letter to the Colossians?

Why do you think he does this?

If you were imprisoned and your life might end any day because of it, would you begin a letter to friends in this fashion? Why or why not?

Reread: Colossians 1:1

Who was with Paul when he wrote this letter?

Reread: Colossians 1:2

To whom was his letter addressed?

How did he describe these people?

What heartfelt wish did Paul express for this special group?

Reread: Colossians 1:3-4

For what two reasons did Paul offer thanks when he prayed about the believers in Colossae?

How would you define faith?

Note: Going back to the original language in the text we see that the faith spoken of relates to more than giving intellectual assent to a set of facts. It involves a deep trust, total reliance upon and knowing on a personal basis.

Was the faith that the Colossians evidenced in a particular religious system, doctrine or philosophy or, conversely, in a specific person?

What is the difference?

Why is the object of one's faith so vitally important?

How do you see the love mentioned in this verse playing into one's faith?

Dr. Charles Missler said that doctrinal correctness will never atone for lack of love. He went on to claim that love, as evidenced in the life of a believer, is "evidence of salvation." This would, of course, need to be augmented by other evidences such the ones we see in Galatians 5:22-23.

What are your thoughts about this?

Reread: Colossians 1:5

What was the source of the hope the Colossians had?

Note: The use of the word "hope" in the Greek is the opposite of our use of the word in English. In the Greek, "hope" is a confidence, sureness, and knowledge of future things. In fact, in the Greek, the word "hope" infers a certainty stronger than knowing. It is an ultimate, internal, overpowering, all-enveloping eternal surety and truth that is absolute.

For how long had the Colossians experienced Biblical hope?

When should Biblical hope become a reality in the life of someone today?

Is there anything one needs to do to maintain this Biblical hope? Please explain.

In Colossians 1:4-5 we see that faith, hope and love seem to somehow go together. How might you explain the way in which this works in one's life? Please think of a concrete example.

Reread: Colossians 1:6

What two things did Paul say the Good News was doing?

Is the Good News still doing these things today? How so?

What did the Good News do for the Colossians?

When did this transformation begin?

What two preconditions were necessary for the Good News to act in this fashion in the lives of the Colossians?

Why was the Good News effective with the Colossians when they understood God's grace?

Note: This also infers that they had been made to understand God's moral law, their breaking of that law and the consequences of their transgression (sin).

Read: Ephesians 2:8-9

Note:

Grace is defined as getting what you don't deserve.

Mercy is defined as not getting what you do.

Why was it necessary for the Colossians to understand the gravity of their situation before they fully appreciated God's gift to them?

One of the great legal minds and students of history of the past two thousand years was John Selden who lived in England from 1584 until his death in 1654. His personal library alone held over 8,000 volumes. Upon his death bed he is reported to have said: "I have surveyed much of the learning that is among the sons of men, and my study is filled with books and manuscripts on various subjects. But at present, I cannot recollect any passage out of all my books and papers whereon I can rest my soul, save this from the sacred Scriptures: "The grace of God that bringeth salvation hath appeared to all men" (Titus 2:11)."

How does this final recorded statement of this learned man impact you?

Reread: Colossians 1:7

From whom did the Colossians learn about the Good News?

What three things do we learn about Epaphras in this one verse?

    1.

    2.

    3.

Reread: Colossians 1:8

What had Epaphras told Paul and Timothy about the Colossians?

If two people like Paul and Timothy were writing about you today, what do you think would be the distinguishing characteristics they would mention?

Are these characteristics things you would like for others to recognize in you? Why or why not?

Reread: Colossians 1:9

When did Paul and Timothy begin and stop praying for the Colossians?

Why didn't they stop?

How might we apply this in our lives today as we relate to other believers?

What three vital things did Paul and Timothy ask God to give to the believers in Colossae? Please make a list.

   1.

   2.

   3.

Knowing the cultural environment in which the Colossians found themselves, why were these particular three elements of such great importance?

Are these three commodities of great importance to believers in the world today? How so?

We can be further benefited by an analysis of the original Greek as it relates to this verse.

First, the Greek word translated "knowledge" is *epignosis*. This is correctly understood to mean "superknowledge," which is in direct contrast to the "superior knowledge" later claimed by the Gnostic heretics.

Second, the Greek word translated "spiritual wisdom" is *Sophia* and means practical knowhow that comes from God. We also see this same Greek word used in the following verses. Please take a look at each reference to obtain a fuller understanding of the import of its use.

Colossians 1:28

Colossians 2:3

Colossians 2:23

Colossians 3:16

Colossians 4:5

James 1:5

James 3:15

Third, the Greek word translated "understanding," both in this verse as well as in Colossians 2:2, is *synesei*. This relates to clear analysis, decision-making and application of *epignosis* to different situations. This is in contrast to the legalistic and unproductive rule making referenced in Colossians 2:23 practiced by false teachers.

The correct application and realization of the knowledge, spiritual wisdom and understanding referenced by Paul in Colossians 1:9 then comes to fruition when it is operant in the life of a believer. This results in the type of stability and surety further referenced in Ephesians 1:4 which says:

"Then we will no longer be immature like children. We won't be tossed and blown about by every wind of new teaching. We will not be influenced when people try to trick us with lies so clever they sound like the truth." NLT

How does this stability of thought and life compare to that of "the world" at large?

A humorous saying I saw embroidered on a dish towel said "you have all the decision making ability of a squirrel crossing the road." The thoughts and actions of a mature believer ought to be the exact opposite of this state of mind.

Reread: Colossians 1:10

When one has the three concepts mentioned in Colossians 1:9 operating in their lives there are apparent results. According to this verse, what are they? Please enumerate these essential components of one's life as a believer.

1.

2.

3.

4.

5.

Does this mean that nothing a believer does should be unrelated to their faith? How so?

Reread: Colossians 1:11-12

What other fruit of one's relationship with God, through the power of the Holy Spirit, does one also need to experience to make their life as effective as possible? Please also list these elements.

Note: Of the last two on the list, one is a state of being and one is a quality of one's life.

1.

2.

3.

4.

5.

6.

7.

Note: Endurance implies that one does not easily buckle under pressure. Patience normally involves some sort of self-restraint instead of hasty retaliation.

It is interesting to note that we often see patience and endurance linked together in God's Word. Please take a look at the following references and note what we learn:

2 Corinthians 6:4

2 Corinthians 6:6

2 Timothy 3:10

James 5:10-11

Please also read:

Proverbs 15:18

Proverbs 16:32

In your own words, how might you describe what happens to a person who does not have endurance and patience?

In practical terms, what seems to be the result when one has both of these qualities operating in their life?

Reread: Colossians 1:13-14

By what means has God enabled people to experience the kinds of lives discussed and dissected so far in Colossians in this session?

If you had to put the ingredients of the means God has used to make this a reality in these two verses in order, how would you do it? Please show the ingredients mentioned in the appropriate order as you understand it below.

1.

2.

3.

4.

Why does it seem necessary that one understand the concepts in these two verses to fully realize and partake of a full life as a believer?

Read: 2 Peter 1:10-11

How might these verses relate to what we have studied in Colossians 1:1-14?

Application Questions

To whom can you write an encouraging letter this week? What will you say and why?

Which specific believers do you feel inspired to pray for on a regular basis over the next month? Why?

What is one specific way you believe you can improve your prayer life?

Close in Prayer

WEEK 2

SUPREME OVER ALL CREATION
COLOSSIANS 1:15-23

Open in Prayer

Group Warm-Up Questions

What person comes to mind when you think of greatness?

What qualities stand out in a person you admire?

Whom do you look up to? Why?

Read: Colossians 1:15-23

Reread: Colossians 1:15

What is Jesus' relationship to God?

Note: Taking Colossians 1:15 out of context has led some people over the centuries to fall into the heretical error of modalism. Modalism teaches that the Father, Son and Holy Spirit are simply different modes of the same being and that there is no substantive difference or separate identity of the three.

However, a holistic reading and understanding of Scripture shows us that the Father, Son and the Holy Spirit are three distinct parts of the Godhead with different identities, roles and functions.

For helpful information on the Trinity I suggest that at a future study one of the group members present a report on the book entitled *The Trinity: The Mystery of the Godhead* by Dr. Chuck Missler. We might also note that Rose Publishing has available a helpful pamphlet on this subject.

In addition, we should realize that following the principles enunciated in "How to Avoid Error" in the appendices of this book will help one avoid mistakes like modalism.

Let us take this a few steps further.

In the King James Version of the Bible the reference to Jesus in Colossians 1:15 is translated as "firstborn." Other translations may use synonyms either as one word descriptors or perhaps several words in an attempt to elucidate the meaning of the original language.

Please take a look at Hebrews 11:17 which says; "It was by faith that Abraham offered Isaac as a sacrifice when God was testing him. Abraham, who had received God's promises, was ready to sacrifice his only son, Isaac," NLT

This particular verse is of import since it shows how in the Hebrew mind prophecy is not just prediction, but pattern. It is a New Testament summary of an Old Testament allusion to the sacrifice of Jesus.

While this is interesting enough on its own, it becomes even more revealing when we look at the verses promised above that tell us about position, place or status of Jesus Christ. It is important that we realize that the original language does not, in Colossians 1:15, refer to time, but to a greater understanding of the power and place of the Jewish Messiah.

In order to make this more clear please read the following references and jot down what we find.

Colossians 1:18

Romans 8:29

Revelation 1:5

Hebrews 1:6

Revelation 3:14

John 1:1-3

John 1:14

John 1:18

John 3:16

John 3:18

Revelation 22:13

Reread: Colossians 1:15-17

The relationship between Jesus Christ, the Jewish Messiah, and the rest of creation is one of grandeur and complexity. Please carefully review these three verses and list what we learn about this relationship.

    1.

    2.

    3.

    4.

    5.

    6.

    7.

    8.

    9.

    10.

Which things that exist were not created by Him?

What impression does this give you of the power imbued in Jesus Christ?

Understanding the unfathomable intelligence and power involved, how should any thinking human being align themselves in relationship to this Person?

Why do people sometimes rail against such an association in the face of the unimpeachable evidence?

Read: John 5:22-29

In what way does this add to our understanding of just who Jesus is?

Read: Romans 1:16-17

How can this immense power impact someone on an individual basis?

Read: Romans 1:18-22

Why do you think some people purposely flail against not only God's great power, but His great gift?

Read: Romans 1:21-31

What is the downward spiral experienced by people who make this irrational decision to oppose the Creator Himself. Please list the things that become evident as noted in these verses.

Note: There are at least 36 of these evidences.

1.

2.

3.

4.

5.

6.

7.

8.

9.

10.

11.

12.

13.

14.

15.

16.

17.

18.

19.

20.

21.

22.

23.

24.

25.

26.

27.

28.

29.

30.

31.

32.

33.

34.

35.

36.

Read: Romans 1:32

What is the negative "icing on the cake" for these people?

What terrible place do they end up on a philosophical and volitional basis?

In our first session we read Galatians 5:22-23. Please read these verses again.

How would you contrast the difference between those who choose to accept the full life offered through Jesus Christ and those who purposely reject it in terms of one's daily life?

Read: Romans 6:23

What is the terrible result of making a decision in opposition to Jesus?

Despite this, what does Jesus offer to those who accept it?

Read: Romans 10:10-11

What simple steps must one take to appropriate a relationship with Jesus Christ?

Reread: Colossians 1:17

This verse says more than most people realize. The Greek word *sunistemi* is translated "consist" or "held together" in many translations. It literally means "to be compacted together, to cohere, or to be constituted with."

To make this more clear please read:

Hebrews 1:2-3 (Please pay particular attention to the statement that "God's Son sustains everything by the power of His command.")

Without going into great detail you might recall the Bohr model of the atom from your high school or college physics classes. This is most interesting since when understood fully there is no real reason why things should hold together. There is some sort of strong nuclear force that makes physical matter consist as what we observe as objects with various degrees of solidity. What is this force? The textbooks don't really know and attempt to explain the phenomena in various ways. However, we have just read, in God's Word, what this force is. Amazingly, it is the power of Jesus Christ that does this incredible work even though most people don't realize it or think about it on a regular basis.

We can begin to see that God's Word incorporates many simple statements of fact that we human beings are only beginning to understand and explain through our primitive attempts at science.

And, speaking of atomic structures and physics, we see another forward looking reference to such things in 2 Peter 3:10.

It can be boldly and surely stated that the Bible is in fact the world's greatest scientific textbook and contains a matter-of-fact picture of historical and scientific reality that people today are only beginning to grasp.

Books can be written upon this subject, but as a matter of interest we might be surprised to observe the following:

- Job 26:7 describes how the earth exists in space before the advent of modern astronomy.

- Hebrews 11:3 tells us about the atoms and molecules, as already noted.

- Genesis 6:15 provides the perfect dimensions for a stable water vessel.

- Deuteronomy 23:12-13 and Leviticus 15:13 teach us about effective principles of sanitation.

- Job 38:16 speaks about springs in the ocean before oceanographers were even born.

- Psalm 4:7 and Acts 4:17 help us understand human emotions and were written prior to the establishment of the field of psychology.

- Genesis 1:20-22 explains the chicken and egg dilemma.

- Isaiah 40:22 tells us that the earth is a sphere prior to spacecraft being able to take pictures of it from outer space.

- Romans 1:20-32 explains that rejecting the Creator results in moral depravity.

- Genesis 7 and II Peter 3:5-6 provide information about the flood that resulted in worldwide fossil evidence and the future irrational denial of this event later on.

- Genesis 1:9-10 teaches that there was one central land mass giving way to the "continental drift" before geographers "invented" the theory.

- Jeremiah 1:5 and Exodus 21:22-23 explain that life begins at fertilization and that killing an unborn child is considered by God to be murder. This was, of course, thousands of years before modern medical research confirmed when life begins.

- Psalm 19:6 explained that the sun travels in a circuit 3000 years before humans figured it out.

- Job 38:35 in the KJV speaks of radio and light waves and their use to transmit speech before the advent of what we consider to be modern communication technology.

- Proverbs 17:22 and 18:14 explain that laughter promotes healing and that a negative attitude has harmful physical effects thousands of years before it was confirmed by psychology and medical research.

- Leviticus 23:22 and 25:1-24 lay down the principles of effective organic pest control and land management before the "modern" environmental movement.

Note: You might enjoy looking up these references to enhance this study and confirm my brief summaries.

Reread: Colossians 1:18

What is the relationship to the body of believers around the world, sometimes called the church?

Note: This is not to be mistaken for or confused with various or particular "churches," or denominations.

How and why is the resurrection of Jesus significant?

Reread: Colossians 1:19

Also read:

Colossians 2:9

Philippians 2:5-11

How did Paul explain the deity of Jesus?

Note: The Greek word translated "fullness" is *pleroma* and indicates that the sum of all divine power and attributes are fully and permanently in Jesus. They were not somehow added to Him.

Reread: Colossians 1:20

What did God achieve through his Son?

How did He do this?

Read: Leviticus 17:11

Why was it necessary for Jesus to shed His blood to do this?

What do you take this to mean?

Based upon the verses we reviewed from Romans today, what must one do to make this a reality in their own life?

Reread: Colossians 1:21

Also read: Romans 5:1

For whom did Jesus sacrifice Himself?

What is one's relationship to God prior to appropriating the power and sacrifice of Jesus?

What is one's relationship with God after this has been done?

If this has become a reality for you, please explain how it has impacted your life.

Read: Colossians 1:22

What has God now done for believers?

Based upon God's action through Jesus, how do believers now appear as they stand before God?

Does it seem strange to you that as a flawed human being you can stand faultless before the Creator Himself? Please explain.

How do you feel about this almost unspeakable privilege?

What difference should it make in one's life when they realize the fullness of what God had done through Jesus Christ?

Reread: Colossians 1:23

Note: Even at this early point in history, false teachers were attempting to move people who had found new life through Jesus away from the truth of the Gospel and His Word.

What two very specific things did Paul admonish the Colossian believers to do?

Why was this so important?

Does this apply to believers today?

What particular thing did Paul warn the Colossians to not do?

Why was this so important and how does it relate to people today?

How firm is your faith?

Note: Depending on the translation of the Bible you are using we can see that the Colossians are encouraged to not move away from the "hope of the Gospel," KJV. The NLT translates this as "assurance." From our first session in Colossians you might recall that the Biblical concept of hope comes from an understanding of the original language. In the Greek, "hope" is a confidence, sureness, and knowledge of future things. In fact, in the Greek, the word "hope" infers a certainty stronger than knowing. It is an ultimate, internal, overpowering, all-enveloping eternal surety and truth that is absolute.

In the case of Colossians 1:23 we must take this a step further because the verse begins with what appears to be a conditional connector. The first word in the verse is sometimes translated "if" and sometimes as "but." A cursory and out of context reading then makes it appear that if believers stand firmly in the truth of God's Word they will be "saved," and if they do not then they will not.

This brings us to the important subject of eternal security. This is a broad and involved issue. However, a review of some of the concepts found in our study on the Gospel of John might be helpful to us as we think about this issue. To that end, let us revisit some key verses and concomitant questions.

Read: John 6:36-40

What promise do we see for those who come to trust in Jesus?

How did Jesus summarize His Father's will?

This passage contains some concepts that are sometimes, on the surface, difficult to understand. We see:

1. God's promise to those who come to Jesus.

2. The concept that one must come to Jesus to receive life.

3. The statements about those who have come to Him and are going to come to Him. (He already knows.)

4. The statement that the Lord wants all men and women to come to Him.

This seeming conundrum can be more fully understood as one studies the Scriptures and views them a whole. In other words:

1. God wants all people to come to Him.

2. We must choose to come to Him.

3. The "elect" will come to Him.

4. God knows who will come to Him.

In theology this is type of occurrence is referred to as an antinomy.

In his book *Evangelism and the Sovereignty of God*, J. I. Packer states that the sovereignty of God and man's responsibility is an antinomy--an appearance of contradiction between conclusions which seem equally logical, reasonable or necessary (p. 18). He continues to say that while God "orders and controls all things, human actions among them . . . He holds every man responsible for the choices he makes and the courses of action he pursues" (p.22).

We can see this borne out in the following verses:

John 17:2

John 17:6

John 17:9

John 17:11-12

John 17:24

Ephesians 1:4

2 Thessalonians 2:13

1Timothy 2:3-4

2 Peter 3:9

Some people find it helpful to think of this in terms of a "life parade." Imagine God, who is not bound by the constraints of time, flying in a helicopter high above a parade of the events that will make up your life. He knows the beginning from the end, He knows the way He wants you to go, and yet you have a choice.

We should also note the importance that Jesus attaches to our resurrection in the passage under consideration in this session.

See:

John 6:39

John 6:40

John 6:44

John 6:54

Why do you think Jesus continues to tell His listeners that there will be a resurrection for those who trust in Him?

What does this mean to you?

Read: John 6:41-44

Who did Jesus say would come to Him?

If we then relate this to the following passages of Scripture, it becomes even more obvious that the <u>endurance</u> spoken of in Colossians is an overt <u>manifestation of the reality</u> that one has in fact placed their trust in Jesus Christ.

Read:

1 Corinthians 15:1

1 Corinthians 15:2

Hebrews 3:6

Hebrews 10:38

Hebrews 10:39

This <u>endurance</u> is <u>objective</u> and <u>observable</u> <u>proof</u> of the reality of one's relationship with God through His Son and enjoyed in the power of the Holy Spirit.

Reread: Colossians 1:23

At the time Paul wrote this letter to the Colossians from prison, how far around the world had the Good News reached?

What was the special privilege given to Paul in relationship to the Good News?

Do some people have this privilege today?

Read: Matthew 28:18-20

Do all believers, in fact, share in this privilege and responsibility today?

What can a person do if their faith is weak? How can they change this situation?

Application Questions

What truths about the power of Jesus do you want to communicate to other people this week? How will you do it?

How can you act to strengthen your faith this week?

Close in Prayer

WEEK 3

ENCOURAGED, UNITED AND CONFIDENT
COLOSSIANS 1:24-2:5

Open in Prayer

Group Warm-Up Questions

When was the last time you had a good physical workout?

How do you feel after strenuous exercise?

Read: Colossians 1:24-Colossians 2:5

Reread: Colossians 1:24

For what reason did Paul say he was glad?

What did he do for the sake of the church?

What, exactly, do you take this to mean?

Do you think suffering is a normal part of life for a person who has decided to follow Jesus? Please read the following verses as you construct your answer and jot down what we see.

Matthew 5:10

John 15:18

2 Timothy 3:12

Hebrews 11:32-40

2 Corinthians 12:10

Philippians 3:8

Acts 5:40

Matthew 7:14

Acts 5:41

Philippians 3:10-11

Reread: Colossians 1:25

What particular responsibility did God give to Paul?

What do you think it means that he was to proclaim "the entire message?"

What might some people have left out of this message?

Based upon your knowledge of the Scriptures and what you see in the world today, what do you think is often left out of God's message from the Scriptures when it is proclaimed?

It has been noted that when Christian missionaries go to a locale seemingly untouched by the Good News they are, in the end, often thrilled to see many people accepting Jesus as their savior.

It has been further noted that when these missionaries used only the New Testament as their text, there are many converts. However, after a period of time problems seem to crop up in the behavior of these new "Christians." Cheating in business, unfaithfulness to spouses, greed, and even lying all begin to rear their ugly heads in the daily lives of the new "churches."

Conversely, when these new believers have made their decisions and studied both the New and Old Testament, that is the Bible as a whole, they have generally lived productive and exemplary lives.

Why do you think this situation exists? What is the reason for this dichotomy?

Ray Comfort is an internationally famous speaker and author as well as a Jew who has figured out that the Jewish Messiah is in fact Jesus. He makes a great point of talking to people and not writing only the new life available to people through Jesus. He also wants to make sure that everyone understands God's moral law as clearly communicated in the Old Testament. His contention is that when someone understands that they personally have violated God's moral law and deserve lasting punishment in hell that they then take things much more seriously.

As a case in point, Ray discusses the way in which many people have made an almost casual "commitment" to Jesus Christ for the perceived experiential benefits and then seem to have "fallen away" when things in life became difficult. He would contend that they never really understood things and they never really did make a commitment.

What are your thoughts about Ray's focus on God's moral law and the results of either understanding it or not understanding it?

This is not to say that God has made some sort of mistake by not including the Ten Commandments in the New Testament. They are, in fact there, although not in the form of one consolidated list. It is, however, incumbent upon us to understand and view God's Word to us as a whole. The New Testament and Old are in many ways separated only by one unnecessary page in the Bible. They flow together seamlessly and do more than simply support each other. They provide to us an integrated message system from the Creator. When taken together they enable one to live a productive and victorious life. (See How to Avoid Error in the appendices of this book for more details about how God's Word works to our benefit when properly used as a whole.)

To illustrate the point about the Ten Commandments being endemic to the New Testament and not simply listed once in the Old Testament please take a look at the references below. (In the New Testament writings the authors understand the importance of God's moral law as enunciated in the Ten Commandments and make either direct, indirect, or assumptive references to it.) Please also note that the following references are only representative. God's moral law is repetitively referenced throughout the New and Old Testaments.

	Old Testament	New Testament
10 Commandments	Exodus 20:1-17	Matthew 19:17
Commandment 1	Exodus 20:3	Matthew 22:37-38
Commandment 2	Exodus 20:4	John 4:24
Commandment 3	Exodus 20:7	Matthew 15:19
Commandment 4	Exodus 20:8	Luke 4:16
Commandment 5	Exodus 20:12	Matthew 19:19
Commandment 6	Exodus 20:13	Matthew 19:18
Commandment 7	Exodus 20:14	Matthew 19:18
Commandment 8	Exodus 20:15	Matthew 19:18
Commandment 9	Exodus 20:16	Matthew 19:18
Commandment 10	Exodus 20:17	Romans 7:7

Reread: Colossians 1:26

To what mystery did Paul refer?

Reread: Colossians 1:27

To what additional group did God choose to make His message known?

Who was in the original group?

(See Acts 11:1-18)

What is the secret spoken of in Colossians 1:27?

Based upon our discussions in Colossians so far, how would you describe the "hope" or "assurance" mentioned in this verse?

Reread: Colossians 1:28

What methodology did Paul use to communicate God's Good News to people? Please explain and list the three steps he mentions in this verse.

Step One:

Step Two:

Step Three:

How is this similar to the pattern utilized by Ray Comfort?

Is this a pattern that we might also use with success? Please explain.

Reread: Colossians 1:28-29

Why did Paul work and struggle so hard?

On what did Paul depend for personal power in the course of this struggle?

Is this same power available to believers today?

Please read the following verses as you construct your answer.

Acts 1:8

Hebrews 4:12

2 Timothy 3:16-17

Psalm 119:105

Psalm 95:1-7

Reread: Colossians 2:1

What did Paul want the Colossians to know?

For whom was he concerned?

Why do you think he agonized so?

Have you ever suffered and struggled on behalf of other believers? Please explain.

Reread: Colossians 2:2

What did he want the people for whom he agonized to know and understand? Please make a list.

1.

2.

3.

4.

How does this tie into the Biblical concept of hope which we discussed previously in our study of Colossians?

What makes a group of believers feel encouraged and united?

How do you feel when you are part of a group of believers that is <u>NOT</u> encouraged and united?

How do you feel when you belong to a group of believers that <u>IS</u> encouraged and united?

Reread: Colossians 2:3

Where, in an ultimate sense, can one find all the hidden treasures of wisdom and knowledge?

How, in practical terms, is this possible? Please explain.

What is necessary in order to make this a reality in one's life?

Reread: Colossians 2:4

Against what did Paul admonish the believers in Colossae to guard?

What deceptive and clever arguments must believers guard themselves against in the world today? Please think of some examples.

What is the most effective way for believers today to be certain they do not fall prey to specious statements, practices, and philosophies?

Please read the following verses as you think about your answer and jot down what you see.

Psalm 119:105

Psalm 119:14

Psalm 119:114

Isaiah 55:11

Psalm 130:5

Proverbs 30:5

Psalm 119:11

John 16:12-14

Hebrews 10:24-25

2 Samuel 22:31

James 1:22

Luke 12:2

John 14:26

Genesis 2:18

Psalm 119:7

Psalm 133:1

Matthew 18:20

Proverbs 27:17

Colossians 3:16

Reread: Colossians 2:5

For what purpose did Paul rejoice?

How do you feel when you learn that believers somewhere else are living as they should with a strong faith in Jesus?

Application Questions

What can you do to encourage and unite the believers with whom you are associated?

What can you do to encourage and unite believers with whom you have no direct personal contact?

What can you do to increase your endurance as a believer this week?

Close in Prayer

VIGILANT, INFORMED AND EFFECTIVE
COLOSSIANS 2:6-23

Open in Prayer

Group Warm-Up Questions

What good advice have you never forgotten?

In what ways would you characterize yourself as tolerant and in what ways would you be considered a hardliner?

Read: Colossians 2:6-23

Reread: Colossians 2:6

What did Paul tell the Colossians they must do after having accepted Jesus as their Lord?

Reread: Colossians 2:7

What two things did Paul tell the Colossians to do as they continued to follow Jesus as their Lord?

What do you think he meant by this?

What specific two things did Paul say would be the result when someone properly builds their life on a relationship with Jesus?

What are some of the characteristics of a tree that is firmly rooted and well nourished?

How does this relate to a believer who is properly rooted in Jesus Christ as Lord?

Reread: Colossians 2:8

How would you characterize the kind of specious, untrue, and false teaching that Paul was concerned about?

What examples of this do you see in the world today?

On an historical basis we should realize that many of those considered to be great philosophers really had no answers to the mysteries of life. For example:

1. Plato was looking for a divine "word" which would come with authority and make everything plain to him. Unfortunately, he was unacquainted with the Word of God as available to him at that time in the Tanakh (what Jews call the Old Testament) on a personal basis or he would have felt differently. See:

   • John 1:1-3.

   • John 1:14.

2. Socrates famously said "It may be that Deity can forgive sins, but I don't see how."

   • Like Plato, Socrates, though well read, was not conversant enough with the Hebrew Scriptures to understand the plan of God.

Bringing this forward to our day and time there are two overriding systems of philosophical thought that are prevalent in the world and self-defeating for their adherents. At the same time they both exist under the banner of the morally relativistic popular religion of our time known as **Secular Humanism**. These two systems are identified as:

1. **Stoicism**, whereby one attempts to live unaffected by the world around him and is therefore somehow superior to it. We see this contrasted in:

   • 1 Corinthians 9:24-27.

   • Philippians 4:11-13.

2. **Epicureanism**, whereby one denies himself nothing that is pleasurable since it all really doesn't matter. We see this reflected in the Biblical record in:

- Ecclesiastes 8:14-17.

- Isaiah 22:13.

- 1 Corinthians 15:32.

Having said this we should realize that nowhere does God's Word condemn knowledge. Quite the opposite is true. In fact, many of the great people in the world of science on an historical basis have either been believers or had great respect for the Word of God. When preparing this material I first thought to include a partial list of such people and the task seemed relatively easy. However, when I began to compile it I ended up with over 200 pages with names and biographies of these intelligent and humble scientists in short order. I still, of course, want to provide people with a list. However, since the list is so voluminous I am limiting it to a number of the more well-known members of the field primarily from history. If you have had a classical liberal arts education you will recognize these people as giants of science. The long list goes on and on. The short list that I put together includes:

1. **Francis Bacon** (1561-1626) credited with establishing what is today called "the scientific method." He founded the Royal Society of London and believed that God gave us "two great books to study:" the first being the Bible and the second being nature.

2. **Johannes Kepler** (1571-1630) codified the laws of planetary motion and is considered to be the father of physical astronomy. He conclusively showed the heliocentricity of the solar system, developed a system of mapping the stars, and was instrumental in the development of calculus. From his study of the planets and mathematics he believed the earth to be

6,000-7,000 years old (which interestingly corresponds with the Biblical record).

3. **Blaise Pascal** (1623-1662) was involved with the development of calculus and composite probability theory. (See the appendix at the end of this study book.) He invented the hydraulic press and mechanical calculator and is credited with the statement that every person has a "God shaped hole" in their heart.

4. **Sir Isaac Newton** (1642-1727) discovered the law of gravity and helped to develop calculus into a separate branch of mathematics. He built the first reflecting telescope and believed the Bible not only authenticates itself but is also the most accurate historical document in existence. He was an outspoken proponent of a literal six days of creation, the flood of Noah and the literal timeline of history as presented in the Bible.

5. **Michael Faraday** (1791-1867) discovered electromagnetic induction and the link between light and magnetism. He was a devout member and Elder of his church.

6. **Samuel F. B. Morse** (1791-1872) invented the telegraph, Morse code, and the first camera in America. He said the older he became "the clearer is the evidence of the divine origin of the Bible."

7. **Louis Pasteur** (1822-1895) was perhaps the greatest biologist who ever lived. He discovered and promulgated the modern understanding of germs and developed many vaccines including those for rabies and anthrax.

8. **Florence Nightingale** (1820-1910) transformed nursing into a respected and highly trained profession. She was a leader in sanitary reforms credited by some with extending life expectancy in the United States by 20 years. Florence was a devout Christian who believed God called her to her work.

9. **J. J. Thomson** (1856-1940) discovered the electron, invented the mass spectrometer and obtained the first evidence for isotopes of stable elements. He also read his Bible and prayed on a daily basis.

10. **William Thompson**, Lord Kelvin (1824-1907) developed the scale of absolute temperatures in use today and codified the first two laws of thermodynamics. He believed and stated that science affirms the Biblical record of Creation and actively debated against the fallacies of Darwinism.

11. **George Washington Carver** (1864-1943) improved agriculture in the United States by promoting nitrogen emitting peanuts as an alternative rotational crop to cotton and thus preventing soil depletion. He was also an evangelist and Bible teacher.

12. **Wernher Von Braun** (1912-1977) helped develop the German V-2 rocket and after immigrating to the United States he led in the field of guided missile development. He ultimately became the director of NASA. Dr. Von Braun said that "the vast mysteries of the universe should only confirm our belief in the certainty of its Creator." He was always pleased to have the opportunity to speak with peers and others about his faith and the Bible.

13. **Francis Collins** (1950-present) invented positional cloning and took part in the discovery of the genes for cystic fibrosis, Huntington's disease, and neurofibromatosis. He directed the National Human Genome Research Institute for 15 years. Most interestingly he is a former atheist turned devout Christian, partially because of his work and realization of the intelligent design inherent in biology.

14. **Ernest Walton** (1903-1995) won the Nobel Prize in physics after he split the atom and proved that E=MC squared. He said that science was a way of knowing more about God.

15. **Albert Einstein** (1879-1955) is credited with developing the theory of relativity and influenced thinking of gravity and time. He was perhaps the best known scientist of the 20th century. His interest in science was motivated by his desire to understand "God who reveals himself in the harmony of what exists." He said "I want to know how God created this world…I want to know his thoughts." He also said "God does not play dice" and most interestingly, "Science without religion is lame, religion without science is blind." Sadly this intelligent Jewish man has never been known to have claimed a personal relationship with God. One can only hope that this became a reality for him prior to his death.

16. **Dr. Jacob L. Rhodes** (1922-2017) gets a special place on my list because he was a personal friend. I became one of his favorite students after organizing an ongoing competition among students in his physics classes to see who could obtain the highest scores on his examinations. After college I became personal friends with him and his wife Ruth, initially when I was working for the Coalition for Christian Outreach, and had lunch with them at their home for many years when traveling through central Pennsylvania. Dr. Rhodes:

- Was a research physicist at Johns Hopkins University and was involved in the development of the atomic bomb.

- Did his graduate study at the University of Pennsylvania, Yale University, the University of Rochester and the Oak Ridge Institute of Nuclear Studies.

- Chaired the department of physics at Roanoke College.

- Taught graduate courses in physics at Temple University.

- Served as chairman of the Department of Physics at Lebanon Valley College for 29 years.

- Most importantly, was a dedicated believer who served as President of the Congregational Council at St Mark's church and as a Bible teacher.

- Most interestingly, as pointed out by our proofreader, Cynthia Nicastro, this brilliant and yet humble man also volunteered at his local library and delivered Meals on Wheels during his retirement.

17. **Ben Carson** (1951-present) was the first neurosurgeon to separate twins joined from birth at the head. He is a dedicated and outspoken follower of Jesus Christ.

18. **Jonathan Sarfati** (1964-present) is a physical chemist and spectroscopist. He is one of the most accomplished and intelligent men of our time having authored at least 16 books and has been featured in at least 14 DVDs. Dr. Sarfati has written hundreds of scientific articles on various topics including those in the fields of apologetics, philosophy, astronomy, natural selection, intelligent design, dinosaurs, ethics, morality, fossils, the worldwide catastrophic flood, Noah's Ark, human origins, the origin of life, and the young earth. He has additionally authored some of the most erudite, cogent and intellectually comprehensive articles and books refuting anti-creationists, progressive creationists and theistic evolutionists. Jonathan currently serves as head scientist for Creation Ministries International and enjoys frequent public debates with those entertaining non-biblical and unsupportable anti-biblical views. Incidentally, he is an internationally known Olympic Chess Champion who has played blindfolded against 12 opponents at once and un-blindfolded against 50 opponents at the same time.

19. **John Hartnett** (1952-present) is a physicist and cosmologist and the author of over 200 papers in peer-reviewed scientific journals. He won the 2010 W.G. Cady award "for the construction of ultra-stable cryogenic sapphire dielectric resonator oscillators and promotion of their applications

in the fields of frequency metrology and radio-astronomy." Dr. Hartnett speaks and writes articles on biblical creationist science with an emphasis on astronomy and cosmology.

20. **Robert W. Carter** obtained his Ph.D. in marine biology in 2003. He is an expert in the fields of marine ecology and genetic engineering and developed new protocols for the rapid cloning of fluorescent protein genes. A prolific writer and holder of many patents, Dr. Carter has authored groundbreaking publications on mitochondrial diversity within modern human populations and cnidarian fluorescent proteins. In particular he produced *Evolution's Achilles Heels*: A unique new book and DVD expose' of evolution's fatal flaws.

21. **John Sanford** (1950-present) He served as a Cornell University professor for over 25 years with more than 80 scientific publications and 30 patents to his credit. A large fraction of the transgenic crops (in terms of numbers and acreage) grown in the world today were engineered using the gene gun technology developed by Dr. Sanford and his collaborators. His groundbreaking book *Genetic Entropy and the Mystery of the Genome* demonstrates why human DNA is inexorably deteriorating at an alarming rate and thus cannot be millions of years old. He founded the non-profit organization Feed My Sheep Foundation.

Scott Gillis, Chief Operating Officer of Creation Ministries International, states that they have more Ph.D. level scientists on their staff than any other organization of its kind. The books and other scholarly work available through this group is second to none in erudition. I heartily recommend every human being visit and study their website at creation.com. In addition, one can view a larger list of believing scientists at https://creation.com/creation-scientists.

There are also a number of interesting publications about unquestionably intelligent and accomplished scientists, who are also committed believers, including but certainly not limited to:

1. 21 Great Scientists Who Believed the Bible by Ann Lamont.

2. Men of Science, Men of God by Henry M. Morris.

3. Scientists Who Believe: 21 Tell Their Own Stories by Eric C. Barrett and David Fisher.

4. Louis Pasteur: Founder of Modern Medicine by John Hudson Tiner.

5. Scientists of Faith: 48 Biographies of Historic Scientists and Their Christian Faith by Dan Graves.

6. Doctors Who Followed Christ: 32 Biographies of Historic Physicians and Scientists and Their Christian Faith also by Dan Graves.

7. Busting Myths: 30 Ph.D. Scientists Who Believe the Bible and Its Account of Origins by Johathan Sarfati and Gary Bates.

8. An article written by Henry M. Morris in 1982 entitled "Bible-Believing Scientists of the Past." Published in *Acts & Facts* and freely available on the Internet.

Note: I suggest you print out and distribute this article among the members of your small group.

Brain power is not lacking here and neither is the humble realization and affirmation of God's truth as presented in the Scriptures.

It most decidedly is not the Bible believing scholars and scientists who have problems with scholarship and veracity.

In light of the preponderance of evidence for Biblical veracity, historicity and truth, how is it that anyone who avails themselves of this data can make the irrational decision to not become a follower of Jesus Christ?

What is the problem that these people face?

Paul himself was one of the most highly educated men of his time if not the most intelligent. He loved knowledge and knew that apart from a relationship with Jesus Christ it was useless. Read what he had to say in:

1 Corinthians 1:30-31

Philippians 3:3-14

How should the information compacted into these verses impact our lives?

In addition, believers are admonished in the Scriptures to know and understand the truth. See:

Ephesians 6:14

John 14:6

2 Timothy 2:15

Reread: Colossians 2:9-10

What three things did Paul affirm about Jesus Christ in these verses? Please list them.

    1.

    2.

    3.

Note: This was already affirmed by Jesus Himself in John 14:7-9 and many other places.

Reread: Colossians 2:11

In what way were the Colossians "circumcised" when they became believers?

Note: This was somewhat of an issue at the time. While circumcision certainly had medical benefits, it was also a sign of the Covenant between God and Abraham's descendants. We see this and its actual eventual intention and fulfillment in:

Genesis 17:9-14

Galatians 2:1-5

Romans 2:25-29

Reread: Colossians 2:12

In what way were the believers on Colossae "buried with Christ" when they were baptized? What do you think this means?

What does it mean that they were then "raised to life?" Please consider the following verses as you construct your answer.

John 14:6

John 10:10

By what power are those who trust in Jesus able to have this experience?

Reread: Colossians 2:13

In what way were the Colossians dead prior to accepting God's gift through His Son?

How did they become alive?

What light does this verse shed on Colossians 2:12?

Reread: Colossians 2:14-15

What four things do we see mentioned in these verses that Jesus accomplished by taking our place in death? Please list these things below.

    1.

    2.

    3.

    4.

Note: Depending upon the translation of the Bible you are using you may see in these verses a reference to "the record of the charges against us" (NLT) or the "handwriting of ordinances that was against us." (KJV) Other versions may say this a little differently. It is interesting to note that this is a reference to the certificate of debt showing the time to be served attached to a prisoner when they were imprisoned. Only when this debt was satisfied would the prisoner be allowed to go free. While incarcerated, the jailer would periodically mark off the time passed until the debt to society in time served was paid in full. When the final time was served the jailer would write *tetelestai*, which means "**paid in full**" across the certificate. The former prisoner would then retain this certificate as proof that their debt had been paid.

We also see this same word, *tetelestai*, in the original language in John 19:30. This is sometimes rendered as "It is finished," but a correct and literal translation is the aforementioned "paid in full."

We might also realize that if a prisoner escaped prior to serving their time and therefore also prior to having their certificate of debt cancelled, the jailer would be responsible for serving their remaining period of incarceration in their place.

Understanding this information about the culture and practices of the time, how might the practices with the certificate of debt and the jailer's responsibility relate to Jesus? Please explain.

Might this connection have been immediately obvious to the Colossians, who were familiar with these practices on a daily basis?

Read: John 12:31

How does this relate to Colossians 2:14-15?

Reread: Colossians 2:16

For what practices are we to not let anyone condemn us? Please make another list. There are at least five.

1.

2.

3.

4.

5.

The issue of the day of Sabbath often comes up in relationship to the two verses we just read. While the discussion of this issue could take several pages, please read the following verses for some general guidance from God's Word.

Genesis 2:3

Exodus 20:11

Deuteronomy 5:15

Romans 14:5

Hebrews 10:25

We might also note:

1. The Jews, on an historic basis, have celebrated the Sabbath on Saturday. See:

   • Exodus 20:8-11.

   • Exodus 31:16-17.

   • Deuteronomy 5:12-15.

   • Acts 15:21.

2. The Jews and converts to Judaism met in the synagogue on the Sabbath. See:

   • Mark 6:2

   • Luke 4:31

   • Luke 13:10-16.

   • Acts 13:14

   • Acts 13:27.

- Acts 17:2.

3. The Sabbath was to be a day of rest. See:

    - Exodus 34:21.

    - Exodus 35:2.

    - Deuteronomy 5:14.

4. The Sabbath command is the only one of the Ten Commandments not repeated in the New Testament. This does not mean that it is therefore unimportant or negated as some people claim.

5. Jesus' resurrection occurred on a Sunday. See:

    - Matthew 28:1.

    - Mark 16:2.

    - Luke 24:1.

    - John 20:1.

6. We see a number (six out of eight recorded) of post-resurrection appearances of Jesus occurring on a Sunday. See:

    - John 20:11-18.

    - Mathew 28:7-10.

    - Luke 24:13-33.

    - Luke 24:33-34.

    - John 20:19-23 and Luke 24:36-49.

    - John 20:24-29.

7. The Feast of Pentecost was on the day after the Jewish Sabbath (Saturday) which means the "church was born" on a Sunday. See:

   • Leviticus 23:15-16.

   • Acts 2:1-4.

8. The early believers seem to have met on Sundays. See:

   • Acts 20:7.

9. It is also true that in the year 321 A.D. the Roman Emperor Constantine declared Sunday to be a day of rest. This may have been to:

   • Acknowledge the fact that believers were generally already celebrating the Sabbath on Sundays.

   • Unite a divided empire and supplant the day the devotees of the worship of the Persian Sun God (Mithraism) held sacred (Sunday) with a Christian Holy Day. Many of the Roman soldiers, especially conscripts from conquered territory in the Middle East, were followers of Mithraism.

10. There is no doubt that there are psychological and physiological benefits to resting one day a week. On a secular basis, most productivity experts tell us that having one day of rest each week:

   • Reduces stress.

   • Boosts the immune system.

   • Improves sleep.

   • Adds years to one's life.

   • Helps one be more creative.

- Helps one be more productive and focused when they return to work.

- Improves short-term memory.

- Prevents burnout.

- Can cause people to better enjoy their job.

Of course, we should not be surprised to learn about the benefits of observing the Sabbath day. The one who created us and the day knew it all along.

Read:

Mark 2:27

Isaiah 58:13-14

What do we learn from these two references?

Reread: Colossians 2:17

How are the rules regarding the practices mentioned in Colossians 2:16 described?

Read:

Hebrews 8:5

Hebrews 10:1

Matthew 5:17

Romans 8:3-4

What do you think Paul means when he says that Christ is the reality of the shadows of which he is writing in Colossians 2:17? Please explain.

Reread: Colossians 2:18-19

Be sure to read this in the NLT in addition to any other translation you are using.

How did Paul describe the people who were trying to upset the believers with false teaching? There are several important characteristics of which we should take note. Please enumerate them.

　　1.

　　2.

　　3.

　　4.

　　5.

　　6.

Do we still see false teachers like this in the world today? Please explain and think of some examples if they exist.

What seems to be the intended goal of these false teachers?

Read:

1 Timothy 2:5

John 15:1-5

How can the important truth found in these verses help out when one is faced with false teaching? Please explain.

Reread: Colossians 2:19

Also read: 1 Corinthians 12:12-27.

What impact does Jesus have upon the body of believers in the world?

How might you contrast and compare this to the intended impact of those we have referred to as false teachers?

Reread: Colossians 2:20-21

What has Christ done for believers as it relates to the spiritual powers of this world?

To whom or what do you think these verses refer to when they speak of the "spiritual powers of this world?"

Reread: Colossians 2:20-23

What are some of the rules of this world to which Paul refers that actually are of no effect? Please recreate his list.

1.

2.

3.

4.

5.

These rules also have important characteristics of which we need to take note. Paul has listed them for us in narrative form. In order to make them as clear as possible, please list these characteristics below.

1.

2.

3.

4.

5.

6.

7.

When it is all said and done, of what use are these man-made rules?

If these rules are so lacking in value, why do so many people follow their own version of them?

When have you seen people following such rules to their own detriment? Please give an example.

Why is it so liberating for a believer to be free of these rules?

How does this freedom make you feel when you think about it?

Application Questions

How can you help a believing friend get rid of their false ideas about limiting man-made rules that hinder their enjoyment of the full life offered by Jesus?

How can you exercise the freedom you have as a follower of Jesus Christ in a positive fashion?

Close in Prayer

RIGHT LIVING
COLOSSIANS 3:1-17

Open in Prayer

Group Warm-Up Questions

What do you consider to be your nicest suit or outfit?

When you are finished with your old clothes, what do you normally do with them?

Read: Colossians 3:1-17

Reread: Colossians 3:1-2

Upon what did Paul tell the Colossians to set their sights?

According to these verses, what is there?

What did he say that the Colossians should not concentrate upon?

How is it possible to succeed in this world and at the same time be focused on the next?

Reread: Colossians 3:3

What is the relationship of a believer to this life? What do you think is meant by this in practical terms?

Where is a believer's "real life?" What does this mean to you?

Reread: Colossians 3:4

Also read:

1 Thessalonians 4:16-17

1 Corinthians 15:51-52

What will happen when Jesus returns?

Reread: Colossians 3:5

What things ought to be put to death in the life of a believer? Please make a list of the primary categories from this verse.

1.

2.

3.

4.

5.

Some of the things on this list might seem to be redundant. However, they are not. There are sometimes subtle and important differences. Please discuss and differentiate between each individual category above as it relates to the others on the short list.

Reread: Colossians 3:6

What is the ultimate result in the world as a whole when human beings persist in these patterns of behavior?

This verse speaks of the individual activities associated with the list above as actual sins. What is the relationship of these sins to the overall concept of sin? Please read Ephesians 2:8-9 as you construct your answer.

Reread: Colossians 3:7

What was the situation in the lives of those who became believers in relationship to the categories mentioned prior to making a decision to follow Jesus?

Why do you think the Holy Spirit has generally listed categories and examples of behavior to this point in today's passage instead of providing a list of sins?

Might this be since people tend to look at a list of individual "sins" and think that while many people might be guilty of committing them, they certainly are not? Please explain.

Read: Romans 3:23

The Scriptures teach everyone deserves death on account of their existence as a sinful person by nature regardless of whether or not they have committed the sins on any particular list.

As we discussed in one of our previous sessions on Colossians, habitual and willful participation in particular sins is evidenciary. That is to say that such a life would seem to be evidence that one has not made a commitment to follow Jesus Christ and put Him in the primary position in their life.

Reread: Colossians 3:8-9

Here we see a list of things that Paul is saying ought to be extinguished in the life of a believer. Please make a list of these particular individual behaviors,

1.

2.

3.

4.

5.

6.

Note that lying receives its own verse. Why do you think lying is so negatively regarded by God? (This is a recurring theme throughout the Old and New Testaments.)

Note: Taken out of context, these verses might seem to indicate that anger itself is a sin. However, anyone conversant with the Scriptures knows that this is not correct. (In this instance, like all others, understanding the Word of God necessitates studying it as a whole. See *How to Avoid Error* in the appendices of this book for more information on this topic.)

For a more complete understanding about anger, read the following verses and note what we learn.

Psalm 4:4

Psalm 7:11

Psalm 86:15

Psalm 145:8

Psalm 145:9

Psalm 145:17

Proverbs 29:11

Mark 3:4-5

Hebrews 4:15

John 2:13-18

Romans 12:21

Ephesians 4:26-27

Ephesians 4:31-32

1 Corinthians 13:4-5

James 1:20

Ephesians 4:15

James 1:2-4

James 1:19

1 Peter 4:8

1 Corinthians 10:31

Reread: Colossian 3:10

What should be happening in people's lives when they become believers?

The fact that Paul exhorts the believers in Colossae to do this infers that a person has a choice in this process. What do you make of this?

What difference does one's background make in their responsibility to follow God's pattern for life when they become a believer?

Read: 1 Thessalonians 5:16-22

Why do you think God gives us the choice and ability to do these things or to not do them?

Read: Romans 12:2

2 Corinthians 5:17

Psalm 51:10

Galatians 5:22-23

What happens when one really becomes a believer and sincerely makes a commitment to Jesus Christ?

Does this change take place immediately?

Does the change in one's life regarding patterns of behavior and individual behaviors take place all at once or gradually and continually? Please explain.

How has this worked in your life?

Reread: Colossians 3:12

What are some of the characteristics that should become evident in someone's life when they become a believer? Please make a list.

1.

2.

3.

4.

5.

Why do you think these particular behaviors are some of the first things that begin to become evident in the life of someone who has trusted Jesus?

Reread: Colossians 3:13

How are we to handle faults and offenses of others in our relationships with them?

Why is this often so hard for people to do?

How would you like other people to respond to our faults and offenses?

Reread: Romans 12:2

What should happen to our faults and offensive behavior over time?

Reread: Colossians 3:14

Note: Before going further we should briefly look at the original language of the text. In Greek there are several types of love. This is delineated by the Greek words:

Eros, which refers to the type of romantic or sexual attraction felt between two people. (*Eros* is the noun for this type of love. When expressed as a verb it appears as *eran.*)

Storge, which refers to the love felt between family members as in a parent and a child. (*Storge* is the noun for this type of love. When used as a verb it appears as *stergein.*)

Philia, which refers to "brotherly" love and is most often exhibited in a close friendship. (The noun for this type of love is *philia,* while the verb is *phileo.*)

Agape, which refers to the self-sacrificial type of deep love that might cause a person to lay down their life to save another person. (*Agape* is the noun form of this love and *agapeo* is the verb form.)There is no higher word for love in the Greek New Testament.

The Bible speaks specifically of *philia* and *agape. Eros* and *storge* do not expressly appear in the Bible, although the concepts are obviously there.

Reread: Colossians 3:14

The Greek word used for love in Colossians 3:14 is *agape.*

What should be the overriding characteristic of the interrelationships between believers?

What impact does it have upon unbelievers when they see the love believers have for one another?

Reread: Colossians 3:15

In this verse we see two types of peace mentioned. Please identify, discuss and differentiate between these two types of peace.

Why are these two types of peace so important in the individual lives of believers?

Why are they so important as believers relate to each other?

Why do you think inner peace as referenced in John 16:33 is mentioned prior to peace between believers?

Is experiencing inner peace that comes from a relationship with Jesus Christ a prerequisite of peace between believers? How so?

Thankfulness is also mentioned in this verse immediately after the principles regarding peace are laid down. Why do you think this is so?

How are the concepts of peace and thankfulness related? Please explain.

Reread: Colossians 3:16

In what other components of a rich and full life as a believer are we to engage? Please list them.

1.

2.

3.

4.

5.

What should one do if they, like me, do not have a great singing voice in regard to the admonition about singing?

Why do you think singing is given a place of importance in this list? How does it impact a person?

Reread: Colossians 3:17

What is the overriding principle that ought to guide the life of a believer?

Why is this principle, when followed, so successful?

Application Questions

What fault do you have that you need to ask God's help in eliminating and turning into something productive? How, in your view, can this be done?

How, specifically, can you be more thankful and loving to those close to you?

Close in Prayer

WEEK 6

PRINCIPLES FOR FAMILIES AND WORK
COLOSSIANS 3:18-4:1

Open in Prayer

Group Warm-Up Questions

If you were to make up a slogan that describes those living together under your roof, what might it be?

If you have ever been an employee, how might your superiors have described you?

If you have ever been a boss, how might your employees have described you?

Read: Colossians 3:18-4:1

Reread: Colossians 3:18

Also read:

1 Peter 3:1

1 Corinthians 14:40

Ephesians 5:22-27

Before discussing these verses it might be helpful to look at the original language. The word translated submission or submit has nothing to do with slavery or subjugation. It is actually a military term and has to do with the fact that soldiers are "arranged under rank." Different soldiers have different functions and there must be a structure in place to be certain everything works properly. One soldier is not by nature better than others. However, every soldier has different functions.

The fact that a wife has a different role in the familial relationship does not mean that the husband is better than her or that she is better than the husband. It simply means that God has ordained an organizational structure that works.

What are wives instructed to do?

What exactly do you take this to mean?

Many people in the field of psychology say that the most important thing a husband needs from his wife is respect. What are your thoughts about this?

Read: Proverbs 31:10-31

Here we learn some of the characteristics of what God considers to be a woman of God. Please list them below:

1.

2.

3.

4.

5.

6.

7.

8.

9.

10.

11.

12.

13.

14.

15.

16.

17.

18.

19.

20.

21.

Why do you think the Holy Spirit devoted so much of Proverbs 31 to some of the characteristics of a woman of God?

Do you think this was to instruct women on how to run a successful household? How so?

Do you think God was perhaps making a point to godly men that they ought to appreciate it when they have a godly wife? How so?

In your opinion, how ought men to show their appreciation to their wives?

As a matter of interest, Larry Norman, the "Father of Christian Rock", wrote and sang a song based upon Proverbs 31:10-31. The lyrics follow. (Used by permission):

I need a woman who doesn't take drugs or mess with men,

Believes the Bible and despises sin,

Lifts me up instead of knocking me down

Follows God instead of running around.

I need a woman who's kind and true

I haven't found her but until I do,

I'll be looking for a woman of God,

A woman with a righteous heart.

I'll be looking for a woman of God,

Who doesn't easily fall apart.

I need a woman who knows the measure of what she's

worth

Stores up treasure but not on earth.

Seeks God's will in all that's done,

And keeps her eyes on the holy one.

I need a woman who's kind and true

I haven't found her but until I do,

I'll be looking for a woman of God,

A woman with a righteous heart.

I'll be looking for a woman of God,

Who doesn't easily fall apart.

The next seven lines are Spoken:

The Bible says - a good wife, who can find?

She's more precious than jewels.

The heart of her husband is glad in her

She clothes her children in purple;

Her lamp does not go out at night.

She is known among the people in the city

And her children shall rise up and call her blessed.

I'm looking for a woman of God,

A woman with a righteous heart.

You know, I'm looking for a woman of God,

Who doesn't easily fall apart.

When Larry died of congestive heart failure a few years ago he had been blessed with godly parents and siblings, a fine son, and many friends. Having been divorced he was single at the end of his time on earth and did not seem to have ended up married to the woman of God he hoped to find.

Reread: Colossians 3:19

Ephesians 5:21

Ephesians 5:18

Ephesians 4:31

What attitude are men to display toward their wives?

Why do you think men are told so specifically to love their wives?

Some psychologists tell us that the primary thing women need from their husbands is love? Do you think these people are right or not? How so?

What are men specifically told not to do as they relate to their wives?

If it is true that love expressed toward one's wife is so important to the wife, why is it so destructive when a wife is treated harshly?

Read:

Hebrews 12:15

Ephesians 4:26

1 Corinthians 13:4-5

Let us assume it is true that men need respect and women need love from their respective spouses. If this is so, how does it impact a couple or a familial group when both parties both provide what is most needed to their spouse and the spouse shows appreciation for it?

Can you think of an example where this mutually beneficial relationship seems to exist? Please give an example.

Based upon our discussion so far today, does a happy marriage automatically result when two believers tie the knot, or must they continually work to build it into God's plan for such unions guided by His Word? Please explain.

Reread: Colossians 3:20

Also read:

Exodus 20:12

Leviticus 19:3

Proverbs 6:20

Matthew 19:19

Ephesians 6:1-3

What are children told to do?

Why do you think this pleases the Lord?

Reread: Colossians 3:21

What are fathers told to not do?

Why do you think the Holy Spirit finds it necessary to tell fathers what not to do instead of what to do in this verse?

What is the negative impact upon children when their fathers do not treat them well?

Why do you think it is fathers and not mothers who are told how not to treat their children?

When fathers mistreat their children, why is it then difficult for children to obey them?

Can it, in fact, be necessary for a child to disobey an abusive father?

Why is it that an abusive father in particular seems to leave such scars upon his children?

Why is it that the scars left by an abusive parent seem to only be properly healed through a relationship with Jesus Christ?

Why do you think that coaches who are encouraging are more respected by those they coach than those who berate their charges?

Can you think of any positive or negative examples of this that you have seen?

Looking at the next verses, we find reference made to slaves and masters. Most people reading this material will, however, hopefully not be in a slave/master relationship. They will more likely find themselves in an employer/employee relationship and for that reason we will concentrate on those interactions. However, if anyone using this material is in a master/slave relationship, and these things do still persist in great number in certain places today, we can know that the verses apply quite directly to their situation.

As we read these verses we should not sit in judgement upon the people to which they were written. Slavery was an accepted part of the culture when the books of the Old and New Testament were written so it is naturally addressed in God's Word. It is hard to think of slavery in anything but negative terms for someone who is today free. That being said, we should realize that in some circumstances both slaves and slave owners two thousand years ago had a different experience than that which we might expect.

At the time Paul wrote this letter to the believers in Colossae it is estimated that there were approximately 60 million slaves in the world. Many of these slaves were well-educated and carried great responsibility in the homes of the wealthy and even in the halls of government. In many households such trusted and learned slaves helped to discipline and educate the children as well as to assist in the running of the home itself. They were often well-treated and in many cases voluntarily attached themselves to the household on a permanent basis when offered freedom. (See Exodus 21:5-6)

Of course, not all slaves at the time had an experience like this. Many were ill-treated, beaten, and considered to be no more a possession than that of a cow or horse. However, a godly person treated their slaves differently to begin with. And, as more and more people became believers, many of them slaves and masters themselves, the whole fabric of society began to change. It has been as a result of the action of committed believers that slavery has been curtailed and officially abolished in many areas of the world. You might enjoy the movie *Amazing Grace* which tells the story of this struggle and change in England.

Reread: Colossians 3:22

What primary principles does Paul lay down for those believers who were slaves? Please list them.

    1.

    2.

    3.

    4.

How does this relate to employees?

Something to think about: In what we call the feudal period in Europe, serfs owed their landlord approximately 25% of everything they produced. Today we think of these people as having lived in a state of extreme servitude. At the same time, we each operate under some system of taxation in our respective places of residence. How do we stack up against the feudal serfs?

Reread: Colossians 3:23

What are slaves told to remember as they do their work?

How does this apply to every human being who is a believer today?

Why is it a positive witness in the world today when someone works in this fashion?

Why and how is it destructive to one's witness when they do not follow this admonishment?

Please think of both positive and negative examples of this that you have seen in your life.

What impact did this have?

Reread: Colossians 3:24

What were believing slaves to remember as they did their work?

What should we remember whether we are employers or employees as we do our work?

Why should this spur all believers on to excellence?

The Merriam Webster dictionary defines oxymoron as "a combination of <u>contradictory</u> or incongruous words (as *cruel kindness*); *broadly*: something (as a concept) that is made up of contradictory or incongruous elements."

Some people say that the term "lazy Christian" is, or at least should be, an oxymoron. What do you think?

Reread: Colossians 3:25

What is the consequence for anyone who does what is wrong, most especially in their work relationships?

How does it bring dishonor upon a family when someone does what is wrong in their work relationship? Can you think of any examples?

How does it bring dishonor upon the name of Christ when a believer does this?

This is a much more serious offense than one might imagine. Please read the following verses and note what you observe.

Deuteronomy 5:10-11

Exodus 20:7

Leviticus 19:12

Psalm 139:20-21

Psalm 99:1-3

Matthew 6:9

Galatians 6:7-8

Philippians 2:12-16

What we say and how we say it is also quite important. However, my contention is that not taking God's name in vain involves much more than a slip of the tongue. For a quick reminder of what God's Word tells us about our speech please see:

Ephesians 4:29-30

Matthew 12:36-37

Ecclesiastes 10:12

Proverbs 18:2

Reread: Colossians 4:1

Also read:

Ephesians 6:9

Acts 10:34

Romans 2:11

James 2:1

James 2:9

What final reminders do we find to both masters and employers in these verses?

Why are these things so important to remember?

How does this apply to everyone in life even if they have no employees or slaves?

Might this apply to your relationship with a clerk, a receptionist, a waiter, a person selling you something, or anyone doing something to help you? Please think of some examples.

How does it impact any of the people you just thought about when you respond to them properly?

Read Colossians 4:5-6 when constructing your answer.

Application Questions

What is one way you can improve the way you treat each member of your family?

How can you have an attitude of service to the Lord in your work?

How can you be sure to act right and treat people properly so as to not have taken "the name of God in vain?"

Close in Prayer

WEEK 7

ACTIONS FOR SUCCESS
COLOSSIANS 4:2-18

Open in Prayer

Group Warm-Up Questions

If you had to eat all food without adding salt for the next year, how would it impact your diet?

In your experience, what does salt do the flavor of food?

Read: Colossians 4:2-18

Reread: Colossians 4:2

What prescription does God have for all believers as part of their prayer life?

What do you think it means that one ought to pray with an "alert mind?"

At this point we might take note of several important aspects about prayer.

1. Prayer and watchfulness are never separated. See:

   - Matthew 24:42.

   - Acts 20:31.

   - 1 Corinthians 16:13.

   - 1 Thessalonians 5:6

2. Prayer enables a believer to stand their ground and take the offensive against our adversary. See:

   - Ephesians 6:16.

   - 1 Peter 5:8.

3. We are to pray even about things that we know will come with absolute certainty because of prophecies we see about them in God's Word. See:

   - Daniel 9:2-3.

   - Matthew 6:10.

4. Prayer is an effective antidote to anxiety. It is also purposeful and specific. This goes beyond simply praying about our own situation. It necessarily encompasses prayer for everything, especially including others. It also involves an attitude of gratitude. See:

   - Philippians 4:6.

Sometimes in the "Christian world" prayer becomes somewhat of a casual practice instead of an essential part of one's "walk." Why do you think this sometimes occurs?

Read: Ephesians 6:10-17

This famous passage is about putting on the armor of God. It is of interest to note that without prayer one cannot effectively put on and stay in the armor of God. Why do you think this is so?

Chuck Missler stated "Our walk will directly reflect the time we spend with Him. The soul flourishes in an atmosphere of prayer." What are your thoughts about what Dr. Missler said?

Reread: Colossians 4:3-4

Paul requested that the believers in Colossae pray for two very specific things on his behalf. What were they?

1.

2.

Why were those things so important to him?

What can believers do today to proclaim the message of Jesus as clearly as possible? Please explain.

Reread: Colossians 4:5-6

Also read: 1 Peter 3:15

What guidance do we find in these verses for the successful interaction of believers with the world?

There are several logical steps in this process. Please list them in order below.

1.

2.

3.

4.

5.

6.

7.

Why is this process so effective?

Please think of an example that shows the clout of this methodology.

Note: These two verses can be quite helpful in the daily conduct of a believer if one memorizes them.

For an example of the practical application of these concepts we can look at Paul. For instance:

1. When he went to the synagogue he reasoned from the Scriptures in the manner of a rabbi. See:

   • Acts 17:1-4.

   • Acts 19:8.

2. When he met with the Athenian philosophers at Mars Hill he used his mastery of Greek thought, literature and rhetoric. See:

   • Acts 17:22-34.

3. When speaking with the worshipers of other gods at Lycaonia he used their own practices and understanding to tell them about the one true God. See:

   • Acts 14:11-18.

Reread: Colossians 4:7-8

Who was Tychicus?

How did Paul describe Tychicus?

For what three reasons was Paul sending Tychicus to the Colossian believers?

1.

2.

3.

To the casual reader of Colossians, Tychicus might seem somewhat of an enigma. However, to the first century believers and students of the Scriptures he is much more. Paul had great confidence in him. Looking at Tychicus only through the lens of what is revealed in the New Testament we learn that he was a person who was both faithful to the truth and at the same time caring and concerned for others. We find him:

1. As part of a group of seven people who went along with Paul when he left Ephesus. See:

   • Acts 20:4.

2. Among the men who helped Paul deliver funds from Gentile fellowships to help the poor believers in Judea. See:

   • 1 Corinthians 16:1.

   • 2 Corinthians 8-9.

3. Working with Onesimus to deliver the letters to the Ephesians, the Colossians, and Philemon. See:

   • Ephesians 6:21-22.

4. Going to Crete at Paul's direction. See:

   • Titus 3:12.

5. Going to Ephesus after Crete again at Paul's direction. See:

    •   2 Timothy 4:12.

Reread: Colossians 4:9

What four things do we learn about Onesimus in this verse?

1.

2.

3.

4.

Reread: Colossians 4:10

What do we learn about Aristarchus in this verse?

We can also follow Aristarchus through the New Testament. When we do we find:

1. He was a Thessalonian who was with Paul on his third missionary trip. See:

    •   Acts 19:29.

    •   Acts 20:4.

    •   Acts 27:2.

2. He put his own life on the line in defense of God's Word during the uproar at Ephesus. See:

    •   Acts 19:28-41.

3. He accompanied Paul by ship, likely as a fellow prisoner for the sake of the Gospel, when the boat went through a terrible storm and wrecked. See:

   • Acts 27:2.

4. He is referred to as a "fellow worker" in the book of Philemon. See:

   • Philemon 24.

5. His name seems to imply that he was originally an aristocrat from Macedonia. He apparently renounced his place of prominence to become a *doulos* (bondslave) of Jesus Christ. (This from Chuck Missler's commentary on Colossians and Philemon published by Koinonia House in 1997.)

How was Mark related to Barnabus?

Note: Barnabas was the nickname for a follower of The Way whose real name was Joseph. We see him elsewhere in the New Testament and it is instructive to know that he received his nickname because of his overriding attitude and impact upon the other believers. Barnabas means "Son of Encouragement." See:

Acts 4:36.

How were the Colossians to respond to Mark if he passed their way?

Note: This information about Mark is also of great import. From the historical data available in the New Testament we learn much more about Mark. We find:

1. He was a Jew from Jerusalem and his mother, Mary, was actively involved with the believers in that city. See:

   • Acts 12:1-12.

2. He was there when Barnabas and Saul were on their mission to Jerusalem and left with them afterwards. See:

   • Acts 12:25.

3. He was the subject of a disagreement between Paul and Barnabas when he took a leave from their mission to visit his mother in Jerusalem. Paul temporarily lost confidence in Mark. See:

   • Acts 15:37-39.

4. Mark had apparently redeemed himself in Paul's eyes since their original disagreement. See:

   • Colossians 4:10.

   • Philemon 24.

   • 2 Timothy 4:11.

5. This "redemption" in Paul's eyes was not merely a matter of Mark's actions. It is also a matter of both Paul and Mark growing as believers as reflected in the verses we reviewed earlier in this study regarding anger. It is of particular interest to read:

   • Colossians 3:13.

6. Mark became a trusted companion of Peter and was endeared to all. See:

   • 1 Peter 5:13.

7. While not directly stated in the text, it is widely assumed that the Gospel
   of Mark was written by this same person as Peter's amanuensis. (An
   amanuensis is a person utilized to write or type what another dictates or to
   copy what has been written by another.)

Reread: Colossians 4:11

Note: Today we revere the name of Jesus as above every other name. In the first
century A.D. the name Jesus was common among Hebrews. The name by which
he was called, *Justus*, means a man of integrity.

What do we learn about Justus and the other people Paul has so far mentioned
in today's passage?

Why do you think Paul found particular comfort through the fellowship he
enjoyed with other believers who were Jewish like him?

How does this type of comfort relate to people today? Please think of an example.

Reread: Colossians 4:12

From our first session in the study of Colossians you might recall that Epaphras:

1. Was the one through whose efforts the fellowship in Colossae was founded.

2. Prompted Paul's writing of the letter to the Colossians by virtue of his visit
   to see Paul in prison and his status within the body of believers as a whole.

How was Epaphras described?

For what particular things did Epaphras earnestly pray as it involved the believers in his home fellowship? Please list them below.

1.

2.

3.

Reread: Colossians 4:13

Knowing the cultural and historical situation in which the Colossians found themselves, why do you think Epaphras prayed so hard about the items we just listed?

Why do you think Paul made a point of telling the Colossians about the fervency of the prayers of Epaphras on their behalf twice in the space of two sentences?

For what other groups of believers was Epaphras praying?

Reread: Colossians 4:14

Which other Gentile believers did Paul mention as sending their greetings to the Colossians?

What else do you recall about Luke?

Clue: His name and book have been famous for over two centuries.

Reread: Colossians 4:15

To whom did Paul send personal greetings?

What do we learn about Nympha in this verse?

We might note that in the first century A.D. the fellowships, often called churches, met in the homes of believers. See:

1 Corinthians 16:19.

Romans 16:3-5.

Philemon 1-2.

These small groups of believers have been the real backbone of those following Jesus Christ throughout history. This is not to negate the role and function of larger organizations, but it is to highlight a vital component of personal spiritual growth. Chuck Missler, one of the most intelligent, well-read, and influential Bible teachers of the past quarter century recently passed away on May 1, 2018. He said he experienced more personal growth as a part of the small groups in which he was privileged to participate than through any other venue.

By virtue of the fact that you are using this material I assume that you are also privileged to be part of such a mutually supportive and beneficial Biblically-based group. If you have not had that pleasure, I suggest you either find or start one.

What growth have you experienced on a personal basis as a part of a Biblically-based small group?

If you are not part of such a small group, what growth do you think you might enjoy by taking part in one?

Reread: Colossians 4:16

What instructions did Paul give to the Colossians regarding the letter he sent to them?

    1.

    2.

Note: Many people have wondered about this letter "from" Laodicea. The verbiage here may be telling. Some scholars believe that the letter "from" Laodicea may actually be what we know as the book of Ephesians. Either way, it seems to have functioned as a circular letter to the churches in the region.

Reread: Colossians 4:17

Also read: Philemon 1-2

Archippus is also mentioned prominently in the letter to Philemon and appears to have been the pastor or leader of their group. It also appears that he may have settled down to an easy and comfortable existence in this role.

Why is this sometimes a problem for those who have decided upon a "career in the field of religion?"

Have you seen any examples of a person weighed down in effectiveness by this problem?

Conversely, what examples have you seen of a person who has been "all in" for the cause of Jesus both in attitude and action? How do you explain the difference between the two?

What very specific instructions did Paul send to Archippus?

Why do you think the Holy Spirit found it necessary to extend this message to Archippus through Paul?

Read Romans 14:12

What should Archippus have considered and any other believing leader consider today when taking inventory of their life?

Reread: Colossians 4:18

What did Paul ask the Colossians to remember?

Why do you think he waited until the last passage in his letter to even mention his own personal predicament in which a painful death was a constant possibility?

What was Paul's final wish for the Colossians?

What does it tell you about the character and courage of Paul when we see how he ended this letter?

Paul obviously understood the importance of teamwork between believers in different fellowships for the effective communication of the Good News to the world around him. Is this still important today? Please explain.

What happens when believers from different places or fellowships work together toward common goals for the kingdom of God? Please give an example.

What happens when believers are unable to work together? Please also think of an example of this sad state of affairs.

Paul spoke well of his fellow believers. In fact in his letters he makes favorable mention of over 100 other believers. Why is it important that we also do the same?

What happens when believers fight among themselves and present a disunited front to the world around them?

What kinds of things can you praise about other believers in your interactions with other people? Please give a few examples.

What is the impact when we do this?

Note: This letter, like others from Paul, seems to have been dictated. In this case it appears to have been dictated to Tychicus and Onesimus. When the end of such a letter was reached Paul signed it in his own hand. (All of Paul's 13 signed letters attributed directly to him as well as the letter to the Hebrews close with the word "grace" at the end.) See the following references for examples:

- 1 Corinthians 16:21

- Galatians 6:11.

- 2 Thessalonians 3:17

- Philemon 19

We might also remember that Paul's eye problem may have been part of the reason for this. See:

- 2 Corinthians 12:7.

- Galatians 4:15.

Application Questions

How do you think you can effectively apply Colossians 4:5-6 in your interactions with people who do not yet believe? Please think of at least one specific current situation.

How can you remember to speak well of family members and other believers?

What particular personal relationship can you improve in the next few days? How will you do it?

Close in Prayer

INTRODUCTION
TO PHILEMON

A study of the book of Colossians flows quite readily into a study of Philemon.

From the outset it is obvious that Philemon is one of the shortest "books" of the Bible. It is actually a very personal letter written by Paul when he was a prisoner in Rome to his friend Philemon, who lived in Colossae. And, while it was most definitely personal, the greetings at the beginning and end of the letter seem to indicate that Paul intended it to also be read by others. Certainly, given what has happened on an historical basis, that is what God intended.

To help us better understand the situation as it existed in relationship to Onesimus, Philemon, and Paul we should first examine the issue of slavery in greater depth.

One might ask, how many slaves were there in the world at the time this letter was written and just how common was the practice of slavery? The best estimates available place the population of the world at that point in history at between 200 and 300 million. That is, of course, a huge margin for error. Interestingly, most estimates of the numbers of slaves in the world at the time seem to agree on a number of about 60 million. Doing the math we see that it appears that 20-30% of the population at the time existed in slavery. Just about everyone owned a slave, was a slave, or knew a slave or slave owner. As reprehensible as it may seem to us, the practice was endemic to society at the time.

To get a good handle on this we might think of the population of the world today. If one thinks of the world as a small village with 100 people living within it we would find:

- In terms of geographic origin; 60 Asians, 14 Africans, 12 Europeans, 8 Latin Americans, 5 people from the USA and Canada and 1 from the South Pacific.

- 51 men and 49 women.

- 82 people considered "non-white" and 18 "white."

- 67 people to be illiterate.

- 50 people to be malnourished and one starving to death.

- 33 without clean water.

- 39 without any improved sanitation.

- 24 without any electricity. (Of the 76 who had it most would only use it for illumination after sundown.)

- 7 would have internet access.

- 1 would have a college degree.

- 1 would have HIV.

- 2 would be about to give birth and one would be about to die.

- 33 would be earning and attempting to live on 3% of the combined income of the "village."

- 5 would account for 32% of the earned income of the village.

So what does this have to do with slavery? It simply helps to understand the percentages on a worldwide basis today and to relate them to the time the letter of Philemon was penned. One can slice and dice the numbers any way they choose. For example, in today's world, assume that everyone living in Europe, Latin America, Canada and the United States were slaves and the rest of the world free. The world dispersion in terms of numbers of slaves would then be roughly similar to what it was 200 years ago. As an aside, slavery still exists in the world. WTAE News (Pittsburgh, Pennsylvania) reported on November 18, 2014 that by their estimate there are at least 35.8 million slaves in the world today as defined by "human trafficking, forced labor, debt bondage, forced or servile marriage, or commercial sexual exploitation." Other sources feel this estimate is much too low.

As we discussed briefly in our review of Colossians, slavery was a world-wide de-facto institution and practice at the time this letter was written. While it is true that some slaves had good lives, it is also true that many had a horrible existence. Those with good lives were educated and often charged with educating the children of the household in which they lived and even in managing household affairs. They were trusted to the point that, especially in the case of some Hebrew slaves and slave owners, they voluntarily attached themselves and their family to the household and became bond slaves.

On the other side of the coin, slaves in the Roman Empire were essentially the property of their owners. They were generally treated as possessions much like a cow or other animal. As such, they did have monetary value. Like any other possession a good slave had a high value and a poor one was of not much value at all. The average price for a slave at the time the letter to Philemon was written was 500 denari. This is about how much a common laborer made for one day's work.

However, an educated or skilled slave might be sold for 50,000 denari. These highly valued slaves, such as the ones mentioned who became highly regarded members of a household, sold for 1,000 times as much as a common slave.

Most slaves remained such for their entire lives and their children also became the property of the slave owner when they were born. It was possible for a slave to purchase their freedom or for a slave owner to grant this to them and this did sometimes happen. However, this was not the norm. A good slave was an expensive and certainly very helpful piece of property and most owners did not want to see them leave.

Since slaves were regarded as mere property in a legal sense, and not as human beings, a slave owner could treat them as he or she wished. A slave owner could punish a slave in any way they saw fit. If a slave was rebellious the law permitted the slave owner to put the slave to death with no more fanfare than one today might squash an ant in the kitchen. Sometimes slaves ran away or escaped from their owners. If this occurred the owner could officially register a report with the municipal officials containing the name and description of the slave. The slaves thus placed on "the wanted list" could then sometimes be returned to their owners when caught for a reward.

Knowing this, we can see that Philemon and Onesimus were each in a difficult position. On a cultural basis, when Philemon received back an escaped slave who had stolen from him he would have been within his rights to execute this slave. In fact, societal pressure might have been such that he would have been expected to execute or at the least severely punish Onesimus. Philemon, however, had become a believer through contact with Paul. His life, mind and heart had been changed and at the same time he had to deal with a slave who had "sinned" against him and violated his trust. To get an idea of this one might think of the legal system today. A person in jail for a crime, whatever it might be, may well become a believer. However, he or she must still pay for their crime.

Onesimus, of course, knew that he had been a thief. In his case, his life also had been changed as we see in 2 Corinthians 5:17 which it says "Anyone who is joined to Christ is a new being; the old is gone, the new has come." (Good News Translation) He was, as we see in the Scriptures, a new person. He was no longer a thief. He, like Philemon, had a new nature, a renewed mind, and was now guided by the Holy Spirit which is producing new characteristics in his very nature. As we see in Galatians 5:22-23 this includes love, joy, peace, patience, kindness, goodness, faithfulness, humility and self-control. However, at the same time, he knew he was guilty of what could be considered a capital crime and if he returned to his owner was potentially subject to execution.

WEEK 8

A LETTER TO GOOD FRIENDS
PHILEMON 1-7

Open in Prayer

Group Warm-Up Questions

Who specifically do you know has prayed for you in the past?

How has it impacted you to know that certain specific people either are praying or have prayed for you?

Read: Philemon 1-7

Reread: Philemon 1

Who wrote this letter?

What was the personal position of the writers?

To whom was it written?

How is the primary recipient of the letter described?

Reread: Philemon 2

Who else is this letter addressed to?

Why do you think Paul didn't just send it to Philemon?

Why do you think he purposefully sent it essentially to the entire group of believers in this fellowship?

Might the other believers have somehow helped Philemon in terms of prayer and Scriptural guidance as he considered the decision before him? How so?

In case we missed it, where did the church led by Archippus and Apphia meet?

What similarities do you see between this church and small Biblically-based home study groups today?

Note: To help us keep the players straight we should realize:

<u>Apphia</u> appears to be Philemon's wife. As the woman of the house one of her duties would have been to supervise the slaves. Since Onesimus was a runaway slave she would have had supervisory authority over him while Philemon would have had the final word. Apphia, however, was in a position to exert significant influence over Philemon as he contemplated how to deal with his former slave who left under a cloud and could be executed for his crimes against the household.

<u>Archippus</u> was the leader of this fellowship and many people feel he may have been Philemon's son.

<u>The Church</u>, or group of believers that met in Philemon's house, was also brought into this discussion by way of Paul's letter.

As previously mentioned in this study, the group of believers that met in Philemon's home met in homes of the members. This was true of the other groups of believers, often referred to as churches, throughout the world at that time. (See Romans 16:5 for example.) It was not until about 200-300 years after the birth of Jesus that these meetings began to be held in separate buildings. Over time, these separate buildings themselves began to be referred to as "churches." However, the original and intended use of the term referred to a fellowship and not a building, denomination or organization.

What have been the positive results of this changing use of the term "church" over the ages?

What have been the negative consequences of the changing use of the word "church?"

How do you find yourself using the term "church," fellowship, small group, or other term regarding groups of believers?

Reread: Philemon 3

What two primary wishes did Paul have for the people to whom he was writing?

   1.

   2.

How do you see these two qualities operating together at the same time? Can you think of an example where you have seen them in your life or that of someone else?

Reread: Philemon 4

What did Paul do every time he prayed for Philemon?

Why do you think he did this?

Is this a good practice for us to follow when we pray for other believers? Why or why not?

When do you normally pray in a day or a week?

When do you think you should pray?

Read 1 Thessalonians 5:17 as you construct your answer.

How can one realistically and legitimately follow the admonition in 1 Thessalonians 5:17 in everyday life?

What are the types of concerns, requests or praises that are most often a part of your prayers?

Reread: Philemon 5

What two particular characteristics evident in Philemon's life caused Paul to specifically thank God?

    1.

    2.

Did Paul specifically relate this prayer of thanks to Philemon and not to the whole fellowship of believers?

Was the Holy Spirit through Paul subtly putting some positive pressure on Philemon? What do you think and how might this have been operating?

Where do you think Paul heard about Philemon and his love for other believers? Might it have been from Epaphras, who founded the group in Colossae? See:

- Colossians 1:7

- Colossians 1:8

- Colossians 4:12

Reread: Philemon 6

What did Paul pray that Philemon and the believers with him would do?

There seem to be several components to the fulfillment of this action and it seems that they go in a logical order. Each step would seem to build upon the previous one. Please go back over this verse, reading it in several translations (including the NLT) and:

First, list the logical components.

1.

2.

3.

Second, list these components of what you feel is the correct order.

1.

2.

3.

If it is true that in a human being one of these logical steps leads to the emergence of the next, please explain how this seems to work on a psychological, spiritual and emotional basis.

Read: 2 Timothy 3:16-17

We see that not only is all Scripture quite useful and powerful, but that it fits together like a hand in a glove when we see it as a whole. Knowing this, please read the following verses and discuss how the concepts in them might relate to Philemon 6.

Romans 12:2

Galatians 6:10

1 Thessalonians 5:15

What do you see as the ingredients of a "good" prayer?

When do you think it is good for you to tell someone you are praying for them?

How does it impact you when someone tells you they are praying for you?

How does it help someone when you are praying for them?

Do you think there are things you should pray for and others you should not pray for? Please explain.

Reread: Philemon 7

What aspect of Philemon's persona as a believer had a great impact upon Paul and other believers?

What was the impact upon Paul?

What was the impact on other believers?

Why do you think this particular aspect made such a difference?

How can compliments and encouragement influence someone's life? Please think of some examples.

Why do you think Paul was emphasizing this aspect when he planned to deal with the situation regarding Onesimus later in the same letter? How was the Holy Spirit setting the stage?

Application Questions

Who can you write or call this week to thank for the joy and encouragement they have been to you? When will you do it?

Who in your life is in need of a compliment or other form of encouragement right now? When and how will you do this?

Who are several people you need to pray for this week?

Close in Prayer

WEEK 9

PLEADING FOR HIS LIFE
PHILEMON 8-25

Open in Prayer

Group Warm-Up Questions

What does it take to reestablish trust with someone who has made a major mistake?

Are there some transgressions that a person might commit that although forgiven, still carry with them a sentence that must be carried out? How so?

How or would you welcome back into your home a family member who had runaway?

If you had to ask someone a favor that is so momentous that it might be life changing, how might you go about it?

Read: Philemon 8-25

Reread: Philemon 8-9

Remember: Philemon would have been fully within his legal rights to have Onesimus executed for his crimes against him upon his return to Philemon.

How did Paul introduce the request he was making of Philemon?

What kind of attitude and care did Paul project toward Philemon in making this request?

How did Paul overtly describe himself when making this request?

Note: Paul was nearly 60 years of age at the time he wrote this letter. While some people say that the average age has increased over time the fact is that one's life expectancy has remained fairly constant at 70 to 80 years. (See Psalm 90:10) The average age of mortality has increased, however, because of the decrease in infant mortality.

What other characteristics of Paul and his position were inferred by the manner of his request?

Reread: Philemon 10

How did Paul introduce the subject of his request?

What did he ask Philemon to extend to Onesimus?

What do you think Philemon understood about Onesimus and his relationship to Paul from this one verse? (See 1 Corinthians 4:15 for some potential insight into this question.)

Do you think Philemon might have been shocked to receive this request from Paul? Why or why not?

How do you think Onesimus felt about returning to Philemon?

Why do you think he decided to return to Philemon instead of just continuing on the run?

Do you think Onesimus might have asked Paul to write this letter to Philemon on his behalf?

How do you think Onesimus felt about this letter once it had been written and delivered?

How do you think he felt about Paul?

Reread: Philemon 11

How did Paul describe Onesimus' character in the past as well as his new character?

Reread: Philemon 12

How did Paul describe the way in which he was sending Onesimus back to Paul?

What do you think he meant by this?

What impact do you think he intended this wording to have upon Philemon?

Reread: Philemon 13

What did Paul tell Philemon that Onesimus had been doing?

In what way was Onesimus taking Philemon's place? What do you think Paul meant by this?

What does Paul remind Philemon about where Paul is and why he is there?

Why do you think Paul reiterated these two things to Philemon at this point in his letter?

Reread: Philemon 14

In what fashion did Paul wish for Philemon to make his decision about Onesimus?

Why do you think he wanted him to make his decision in this manner?

Reread: Philemon 15-16

How does Paul describe Onesimus' time away from Philemon?

For how long does Paul say Philemon might have Onesimus back?

In what state was Onesimus when he ran away from Philemon?

In what condition was he returning to Philemon?

Reread: Philemon 16

Also Read:

1 Corinthians 7:21-24

Colossians 3:11

Galatians 3:28

Philemon found himself in an interesting dilemma.

How might it have impacted other slaves and slave owners if he was perceived as being too "easy" on Onesimus in regard to his former transgressions?

How might it have impacted Philemon's witness and ministry if he were too hard on Philemon?

How do you think Philemon should have handled the situation?

Reread: Philemon 17

What does Paul put on the line in making his request to Philemon?

In what manner does Paul ask Philemon to welcome Onesimus back?

Reread: Philemon 18-19

What does Paul promise to do on behalf of Onesimus as it relates to Philemon?

What does Paul remind Philemon that he "owes" to Paul?

Is it safe to say that in a sense Philemon "owes" Paul a debt of eternal gratitude since Paul introduced Philemon to eternal life through Jesus Christ?

Is this in any way similar in pattern to what Jesus has done for you and me?

Read the following verses as you think about your answer.

Romans 5:8

2 Corinthians 5:21

Galatians 3:13-15

Romans 3:24

Does this in any way provide an example that we ought to consider in our interactions with other people in our lives today? How so?

Reread: Philemon 20

For what reason does Paul, in the end, ask Philemon to grant the favor he is asking?

How does Paul say this will encourage him?

How is a person impacted when they successfully intercede on behalf of someone else? Please think of an example.

Reread: Philemon 21

How does Paul "top-off" his request for Onesimus?

What do you think he is accomplishing with this final summary of his request?

Note: This verse is sometimes taken to mean that Paul was asking Philemon to grant Onesimus his freedom. However, this meaning is not in the text. It is an example of what is called eisegesis. Eisegesis occurs when someone imputes their own ideas and opinions into the text under consideration. A sincere student of the Scriptures engages in exegesis, which is doing their best to read out of the Scriptures what God is saying in His Word. (See *How to Avoid Error* in the appendix to this book.)

Since we are attempting to engage in good exegesis through inductive Bible study, let's take a look at what God's Word has to say about slavery in some other places. Please read:

Ephesians 6:5-9

Colossians 3:22-4:1

1 Timothy 6:1-2

Titus 2:9-10

1 Corinthians 7:21-24

Matthew 5:13-16

2 Corinthians 5:17

1 Corinthians 10:31

What guidance do we find here for slaves?

What guidance do we find for slave owners?

What overall guidance do we find for both slave owners and slaves?

Taking this forward to the experience of many people in our day, what guidance do we find in these verses for employees who have trusted Jesus Christ?

What guidance do we find for employers who have found new life in a personal relationship with Jesus?

How should all believers evaluate their actions, words and attitudes?

In what circumstances do you think someone who has become a believer should or should not return to people they knew before their life was changed to rectify past mistakes? Please explain and think of some practical illustrations.

Note: The letter to Philemon was written at about the same time that Paul wrote the book of Colossians.

Read Colossians 3:12-13 to see what Paul had to say about such things in his longer and more general letter to the believers in Colossae.

Reread: Philemon 22

Note: The "your" in this verse is plural indicating that the request is not only to Philemon, but to the fellowship of believers in Colossae as a whole.

What other request does Paul make of Philemon and the believers in Colossae?

What is Paul hoping to soon do?

How does this request seem in comparison to the one he made about Onesimus?

Reread: Philemon 23

Who else is specifically mentioned as being in prison with Paul?

Why do you think he makes a point of telling Philemon and the others in their fellowship that Epaphras is in jail?

Why do you think Paul specifically mentions this person separately from the others sending their greetings?

Reread: Philemon 24

Who else sent their greetings to Philemon and the group of believers that met in his home?

Reread: Philemon 25

What final greeting does Paul leave with Philemon?

How do you think this affected Philemon?

Application Questions

In what way can we help people who have become believers and experienced the changing power of Jesus in their lives?

Is there any broken relationship or promise from your earlier life that you are willing to take steps to rectify this week?

Who needs your affirmation and support as they more fully understand the changes God is making in their life?

Close in Prayer

APPENDIX 1

HOW TO AVOID ERROR
(PARTIALLY EXCERPTED FROM *THE ROAD TO HOLOCAUST* BY HAL LINDSEY)

1. The most important single principle in determining the true meaning of any doctrine of our faith is that we start with the clear statements of the Scriptures that specifically apply to it, and use those to interpret the parables, allegories and obscure passages. This allows Scripture to interpret Scripture. The Dominionists (and others seeking to bend Scripture to suit their purposes) frequently reverse this order, seeking to interpret the clear passages using obscure passages, parables and allegories.

2. The second most important principle is to consistently interpret by the literal, grammatical, historical method. This means the following:

   1. Each word should be interpreted in light of its normal, ordinary usage that was accepted in the times in which it was written.

   2. Each sentence should be interpreted according to the rules of grammar and syntax normally accepted when the document was written.

   3. Each passage should also be interpreted in light of its historical and cultural environment.

Most false doctrines and heresy of Church history can be traced to a failure to adhere to these principles. Church history is filled with examples of disasters and wrecked lives wrought by men failing to base their doctrine, faith, and practice upon these two principles.

The Reformation, more than anything else, was caused by an embracing of the literal, grammatical, and historical method of interpretation, and a discarding of the allegorical method. The allegorical system had veiled the Church's understanding of many vital truths for nearly a thousand years.

Note 1: It is important to note that this is how Jesus interpreted Scripture. He interpreted literally, grammatically, and recognized double reference in prophecy.

Note 2: It is likewise important that we view Scripture as a whole. Everything we read in God's Word is part of a cohesive, consistent, integrated message system. Every part of Scripture fits in perfectly with the whole of Scripture if we read, understand, and study it properly.

Note 3: Remember to Appropriate the power of The Holy Spirit.

Read: Luke 11:11-13   Read: I Timothy 4:15-16
Read: Luke 24:49   Read: II Peter 2:1
Read: John 7:38-39   Read: Mark 13:22
Read: John 14:14-17, 26

APPENDIX 2

UNDERSTANDING COMPOSITE PROBABILITY AND APPLYING IT TO THE JUDEO-CHRISTIAN SCRIPTURES

Before proceeding we might briefly reflect upon the reliability of the Judeo-Christian Scriptures. All honest researchers into their veracity have found that, as historical documents, they are without parallel. They are the most reliable and incontrovertibly accurate documents available in the world today. This has been the conclusion of all the erudite scholars and investigators who have taken the time to delve into this topic. For more information on this subject you may wish to read *The Case For Christ* by Lee Stroebel, *More Than a Carpenter* by Josh McDowell, and the *Evidence That Demands a Verdict* series, also by Josh McDowell. This is, of course, a very short list of the volumes available. A great deal of augmentative and corroborative material is available in such volume that if one were so inclined they might spend a lifetime in its study.

To better understand one of the ways the Creator of the Universe has validated His Word and the work and person of Jesus Christ, it is helpful to get a grasp on composite probability theory and its application to the Judeo-Christian Scriptures.

We are indebted to Peter W. Stoner, past chairman of the Department of Mathematics and Astronomy at Pasadena City College as well as to Dr. Robert C. Newman with his Ph.D. in astrophysics from Cornell University for the initial statistical work on this topic. Their joint efforts on composite probability theory were first published in the book *Science Speaks.*

Composite Probability Theory

If something has a 1 in 10 chance of occurring, that is easy for us to understand. It means that 10 percent of the time, the event will happen. However, when we calculate the probability of several different events occurring at the same time, the odds of that happening increase exponentially. This is the basic premise behind composite probability theory.

If two events have a 1 in 10 chance of happening, the chance that both of these events will occur is 1 in 10 x 10, or 1 in 100. To show this numerically this probability would be 1 in 10^2, with the superscript indicating how many tens are being multiplied. If we have 10^3, it means that we have a number of 1000. Thus 10^4 is equivalent to 10,000 and so on. This is referred to as 10 to the first power, 10 to the second power, 10 to the third power, and so on.

For example, let's assume that there are ten people in a room. If one of the ten is left handed and one of the ten has red hair, the probability that any one person in the room will be left handed and have red hair is one in one hundred.

We can apply this model to the prophecy revealed in the Bible to figure out the mathematical chances of Jesus' birth, life and death, in addition to many other events occurring in the New Testament by chance. To demonstrate this, we will consider eight prophecies about Jesus and assign a probability of them occurring individually by chance. To eliminate any disagreement, we will be much more limiting than is necessary. Furthermore, we will use the prophecies that are arguably the most unlikely to be fulfilled by chance. I think you will agree that in doing so, we are severely handicapping ourselves.

1. The first prophecy from Micah 5:2 says, "But you, O Bethlehem Ephrathah, are only a small village in Judah. Yet a ruler of Israel will come from you, one whose origins are from the distant past" (NLT). This prophecy tells us that the Messiah will be born in Bethlehem. What is the chance of that actually occurring? As we consider this, we also have to ask: What is the probability that anyone in the history of the world might be born in this obscure town? When we take into account all of the people who ever lived, this might conservatively be 1 in 200,000.

Amazingly, about 700 years after this prophecy was uttered it was fulfilled when Yeshua HaMaschiach (The Jewish Messiah), who we call Jesus, was born in exactly the place predicted. We see this in Luke 2:11 where it states "The Savior— yes, the Messiah, the Lord—has been born today in Bethlehem, the city of David!"

2. Let's move on to the second prophecy in Zechariah 9:9: "Rejoice greatly, O people of Zion! Shout in triumph, O people of Jerusalem! Look, your King is coming to you. He is righteous and victorious, yet He is humble, riding on a donkey---even on a donkey's colt" (NLT). For our purposes, we can assume the chance that the Messiah (the King) riding into Jerusalem on a donkey might be 1 in 100. But, really, how many kings in the history of the world have actually done this?

The fulfillment of this particular prophecy 500 years later was so unnerving that Matthew, Mark, Luke and John all included it in their historical accounts.

Matthew recorded it as "Tell the people of Jerusalem, 'Look, your King is coming to you. He is humble, riding on a donkey— riding on a donkey's colt' " (Matthew 21:5 NLT).

This appears in John's writings as "The next day, the news that Jesus was on the way to Jerusalem swept through the city. A large crowd of Passover visitors took palm branches and went down the road to meet him. They shouted, "Praise God! Blessings on the one who comes in the name of the LORD! Hail to the King of Israel!" Jesus found a young donkey and rode on it, fulfilling the prophecy that said: "Don't be afraid, people of Jerusalem. Look, your King is coming, riding on a donkey's colt" (John 12:12–15 NLT).

3. The third prophecy is from Zechariah 11:12: "I said to them, 'If you like, give me my wages, whatever I am worth; but only if you want to.' So they counted out for my wages thirty pieces of silver" (NLT). What is the chance that someone would be betrayed and the price of that betrayal would be thirty pieces of silver? For our purposes, let's assume the chance that anyone in the history of the world would be betrayed for thirty pieces of silver might be 1 in 1,000.

As unlikely as it may have seemed on the surface, this prediction was fulfilled approximately 500 years later and was noted by Matthew with the language itself being eerily similar to what had been written so many years ago. The NLT shows this as "How much will you pay me to betray Jesus to you? And they gave him thirty pieces of silver." (Matthew 26:15) How shocking would it be if you found that someone predicted exactly what you were going to spend for your next dinner out 500 years ago?

4. The fourth prophecy comes from Zechariah 11:13: "And the Lord said to me, 'Throw it to the potter'---this magnificent sum at which they valued me! So I took the thirty coins and threw them to the potter in the Temple of the Lord" (NLT). Now we need to consider what the chances would be that a temple and a potter would be involved in someone's betrayal. For our statistical model, let's assume this is 1 in 100,000.

This prophecy and its fulfillment is a continuation and completion of the one immediately prior to it in which the exact amount of the bribe for the betrayal of the Jewish King was predicted, again 500 years before it occurred. Here we find predicted not only the betrayal and the exact payment, but the actual usage of the funds. Matthew records fulfillment of this whole process as "I have sinned," he declared, "for I have betrayed an innocent man." "What do we care?" they retorted. "That's your problem." Then Judas threw the silver coins down in the Temple and went out and hanged himself. The leading priests picked up the coins. "It wouldn't be right to put this money in the Temple treasury," they said, "since it was payment for murder." After some discussion they finally decided to buy the potter's field, and they made it into a cemetery for foreigners (Matthew 27:4-7 NLT).

5. The fifth prophecy in Zechariah 13:6 reads: "And one shall say unto him, What are these wounds in thine hands? Then he shall answer, Those with which I was wounded in the house of my friends" (KJV). The question here is, "How many people in the history of the world have died with wounds in their hands?" I believe we can safely assume the chance of any person dying with wounds in his or her hands is somewhat greater than 1 in 1,000.

Again, 500 years later we see this specific prophecy fulfilled and the evidence viewed by Jesus's disciples in John 20:20 where it says "As he spoke, he showed them the wounds in his hands and his side. They were filled with joy when they saw the Lord" (NLT)!

6. The sixth prophecy in Isaiah 53:7 states, "He was oppressed and treated harshly, yet he never said a word. He was led like a lamb to the slaughter. And as a sheep is silent before the shearers, he did not open his mouth" (NLT). This raises a particularly tough question. How many people in the history of the world can we imagine being put on trial, knowing they were innocent, without making one statement in their defense? For our statistical model, let's say this is 1 in 1,000, although it is pretty hard to imagine.

In this case, approximately 700 years passed between the time the prediction was made and we see it fulfilled in Mark 15:3-5. There it is recorded as "Then the leading priests kept accusing him of many crimes, and Pilate asked him, "Aren't you going to answer them? What about all these charges they are bringing against you?" But Jesus said nothing, much to Pilate's surprise" (NLT).

7. Moving on to the seventh prophecy, Isaiah 53:9 says "He had done no wrong and had never deceived anyone. But he was buried like a criminal; he was put in a rich man's grave" (NLT). Here we need to consider how many people, out of all the good individuals in the world who have died, have died a criminal's death and been buried in a rich person's grave. These people died out of place. (Some might also infer that they were buried out of place, though that is not necessarily true.) Let's assume the chance of a good person dying as a criminal and being buried with the rich is about 1 in 1,000.

Again we find that 700 years passed between the prediction of this event and the actual occurrence. Again, this event was so momentous that it was recorded by Matthew, Mark, Luke and John. Astonishingly, we find that he was placed in the tomb by not just one person of wealth, but by two. Joseph of Arimathea and Nicodemus, two of the wealthiest men in the region, worked together and laid the body in Joseph's own tomb. Matthew 27:60, speaking of Joseph of Arimathea's part in entombing Jesus' body says "He placed it in his own new tomb, which had been carved out of the rock. Then he rolled a great stone across the entrance and left" (NLT).

8. The eighth and final prophecy is from Psalm 22:16: "My enemies surround me like a pack of dogs; an evil gang closes in on me. They have pierced my hands and feet" (NLT). Remember this passage and all the other prophetic references to the crucifixion were written before this form of execution was invented. However, for our purposes, we just need to consider the probability of someone in the history of the world being executed by crucifixion. Certainly, Jesus wasn't the only person killed by being crucified. We will say that the chances of a person dying from this specific form of execution to be at 1 in 10,000.

Here we might note that Psalm 22 was penned by King David approximately 1000 years prior to the birth of Jesus. The word "crucifixion" and its derivatives had not yet been coined, but we see the process described in detail. Again, because of the import of this event it is recorded by each of the Gospel writers. In Mark 16:6 we see the fulfillment of the ancient prophecy and more where we read "Don't be alarmed. You are looking for Jesus of Nazareth, who was crucified. He isn't here! He is risen from the dead! Look, this is where they laid his body" (NLT).

Calculating the Results

To determine the chance that all these things would happen to the same person by chance, we simply need to multiply the fraction of each of the eight probabilities. When we do, we get a chance of 1 in 10^{28}. In other words, the probability is 1 in 10,000,000,000,000,000,000,000,000,000.

Would you bet against these odds?

Unfortunately, there is another blow coming for those who do not believe the Bible is true or Jesus is who He said He was. There are not just eight prophecies of this nature in the Bible that were fulfilled in Jesus Christ------there are *more than three hundred* such prophecies in the Old Testament. The prophecies we looked at were just the ones that we could *most easily* show fulfilled.

If we deal with only forty-eight prophecies about Jesus, based on the above numbers, the chance that Jesus is not who He said He was or the Bible is not true is 1 in 10^{168}. This is a larger number than most of us can grasp (though you may want to try to write it sometime). To give you some perspective on just how big this number is, consider these statistics from the book *Science Speaks* by Peter Stoner:

- If the state of Texas were buried in silver dollars two feet deep, it would be covered by 10^{17} silver dollars.

- In the history of the world, only 10^{11} people have supposedly ever lived. (I don't know who counted this.)

- There are 10^{17} seconds in 1 billion years.

- Scientists tell us that there are 10^{66} atoms in the universe and 10^{80} particles in the universe.

- Looking at just forty-eight prophecies out of more than three hundred, there is only a 1 in 10^{168} chance of Jesus not being who He said He was or of the Bible being wrong.

In probability theory, the threshold for an occurrence being absurd---translate that as "impossible"---is only 10^{50}. No thinking person who understands these probabilities can deny the reality of our faith or the Bible based on intellect. Every person who has set out to disprove the Judeo-Christian Scriptures on an empirical basis has ended up proving the Bible's authenticity and has, in most cases, become a believer.

These facts are more certain than any others in the world. However, not everyone who has come to realize the reliability and reality of these documents has become a believer. These intelligent people who understand the statistical impossibility that Jesus was not who He claimed to be and who yet do not make a decision for Christ are not senseless; they generally just have other issues. They allow these issues to stop them from enjoying the many experiential benefits that God offers them through His Word and the dynamic relationship they could have with Him, not to mention longer-term benefits. These people, of course, deserve love and prayer, because this is not just a matter of the intellect. If it were, every intelligent inquirer would be a believer. Rather, it is very much a matter of the heart, the emotions, and the spirit.

The truth of this statement was brought home to me in one very poignant situation. In this case, someone very near and dear to me said, "But Dad, this could have been anybody." No, this could not have been just anybody. The chance these prophecies could have been fulfilled in one person is so remote as to be absurd. That is impossible. Only one person in human history fulfilled these prophecies and that person is Jesus Christ. To claim otherwise is not intelligent, it is not smart, it is not well-considered, and it is not honest. It may be emotionally satisfying, but in all other respects it is self-delusional.

Printed in the United States
By Bookmasters